MW00837372

Infrastructure as Code with Azure Bicep

Streamline Azure resource deployment by bypassing ARM complexities

Yaser Adel Mehraban

BIRMINGHAM—MUMBAI

Infrastructure as Code with Azure Bicep

Group Product Manager: Rahul Nair
Publishing Product Manager: Niranjan Naikwadi
Senior Editor: Athikho Sapuni Rishana
Content Development Editor: Sayali Pingale
Technical Editor: Shruthi Shetty
Copy Editor: Safis Editing
Associate Project Manager: Neil Dmello
Proofreader: Safis Editing
Indexer: Sejal Dsilva
Production Designer: Sinhayna Bais
Marketing Co-Ordinator: Nimisha Dua

First published: December 2021

Production reference: 1151221

Published by Packt Publishing Ltd.
Livery Place
35 Livery Street
Birmingham
B3 2PB, UK.

ISBN 978-1-80181-374-7

www.packt.com

To my wife, Rosa, for her sacrifices and for exemplifying the power of determination. To my mom, Sedigheh; there are no words that can express how I feel, and I thank you for what you made me. And to my two little angels, Ronika and Elika; please listen to what your mom says.

– Yas

Foreword

It's hard to overstate the benefits of defining your solution's **Infrastructure as Code** (**IaC**). Continuous delivery, continuous testing, quality control gates, automated security testing, and automated performance testing all benefit from having an automated approach to working with infrastructure.

Until recently, the gold standard of IaC on Azure has been ARM templates. It's fair to say that nobody particularly likes working with its arcane JSON syntax. As a result, it's been difficult for Azure customers to unlock all of the benefits of IaC. But with the introduction of Bicep, defining IaC for Azure hasn't just become easier – it's become fun.

In this book, Yas has taken his wealth of experience and combined a tutorial of the Bicep language with reference material covering its keywords and syntax. There is a lot of practical advice, too, with tips for using the Bicep tooling for Visual Studio Code and the Bicep linter. And to really get the best out of Bicep and IaC, look at the chapters about deployment pipelines and some recommended practices for writing good code.

I often say that Bicep has changed the game of Azure deployments. After you read this book, you'll have a solid foundation for planning your own automated deployment process for Azure.

– *John Downs*

Senior Customer Experience Engineer at Microsoft

It comes as no surprise that Yas has decided to put pen to paper and produce this book on IaC with Azure Bicep. As you read this, what will become evident is his passion for technology, innovation, and for helping people and organizations be their best. I have had the pleasure of working with Yas as his manager and seen his passion firsthand. He has an amazing way of breaking down the complex, evoking thought, discussion, encouraging ideas, and promoting self-belief. This stems from his upbringing and desire to achieve and bring out the best in himself and turn dreams into reality, with no better example of now achieving his goal of one day working for Microsoft.

I know you will enjoy the book as much as I have. You will be inspired by the level of detail and benefit from Yas's shared expertise.

– Edmondo Rosini

Director, Azure Technical Training at Microsoft

Contributors

About the author

Yaser Adel Mehraban is a self-taught and motivated software engineer and solution architect who lives in the most livable city in the world, Melbourne, Australia. He is currently working as an Azure technical trainer for Microsoft. Some might know him as the almond croissant addict cleverly disguised as a successful web developer.

He has over a decade of experience working in a variety of different teams and has helped them adapt DevOps and IaC to be able to increase team productivity when it comes to cloud resource deployment. Furthermore, he has a true passion for sharing knowledge, which has motivated him to give many international conference talks, write hundreds of technical blog posts, and publish courses on platforms such as Pluralsight.

When he is not working, he mostly spends his time with his family or on his woodworking projects, which vary depending on how much space is left in the house.

– I would like to thank Niranjan (project manager) who approached me at the start and has supported me throughout the entire writing process. In addition, I would like to thank Neil (project manager and editor) and Sayali (editor) for their dedication and support to help me write this book smoothly from start to finish. Also, thanks to the technical reviewers, Vaibhav and Alessandro, for their help in spotting my mistakes and validating the technical aspects, which adds so much to the book's practicality. And finally, thanks to my dear friends, John and Edmondo, who have expressed their support through their precious words about me and the book.

About the reviewer

Vaibhav Gujral is a thought leader and a seasoned cloud architect with over 15 years of extensive experience working with several global clients spanning multiple industries. In his current role, he is responsible for envisioning and creating enterprise cloud strategy and continually building and improving the cloud platform foundations that development teams build upon. Born and brought up in India, he has been based out of Omaha, NE, since 2016. Vaibhav holds a bachelor of engineering degree and is a Microsoft Azure MVP. He is also a Microsoft Certified Trainer and holds numerous Azure role-based certifications. He is a regular speaker at several user groups and conferences, and he also runs the Omaha Azure user group.

– I'd like to thank my wife, Geeta, and our two children, Saanvi and Rihaan, for their daily support and patience. I'd like to thank my parents, siblings, relatives, friends, and mentors for their guidance and continued support. Finally, I'd also like to thank Packt Publishing for the opportunity to review this book.

Table of Contents

6

Using Parameters, Variables, and Template Functions

7

Understanding Expressions, Symbolic Names, Conditions, and Loops

8

Defining Modules and Utilizing Outputs

Section 3: Deploying Azure Bicep Templates

9

Deploying a Local Template

10
Deploying Bicep Using Azure DevOps

11
Deploying Bicep Templates Using GitHub Actions

12

Exploring Best Practices for Future Maintenance

Index

Other Books You May Enjoy

Preface

The idea to write this book hit me when Azure Bicep was released and after working with ARM templates for quite a while to deploy resources on Microsoft Azure. I truly believe resource deployment should not be complex and infrastructure as code is a must-have for every organization.

In this book, you will start with some basics and a review of Azure ARM templates and why there was a need for a revision to remove some barriers and make it easier for cloud engineers and DevOps teams to deploy their resources using code. From installation to writing your first template in your local development environment, testing, and deploying it locally, you will learn it all. You will find out about Bicep's syntax and how to write maintainable and reusable templates that can be used in your continuous deployment pipelines with ease. And at the end of the book, there are some of the best practices and industry standards that you need to be aware of.

The book is structured in a way that goes from basics to advanced topics so that you will not have any problems following along even if you have not had prior experience with Azure ARM templates or resource deployments via templates before.

Who this book is for

This book targets cloud engineers, DevOps teams, and developers who are responsible for creating their infrastructure as code (IoC) to deploy their resources in their Azure environment.

What this book covers

Chapter 1, An Introduction to Azure Bicep, describes what Azure Bicep is, why it was created, and some of the goals it's trying to achieve.

Chapter 2, Installing Azure Bicep, covers how to install Azure Bicep on different operating systems along with the Azure CLI and Azure PowerShell.

Chapter 3, Authoring Experience, is all about the developer experience when writing Bicep templates in their local development, especially when using Visual Studio Code and its Bicep extension.

Chapter 4, Compiling and Decompiling Bicep Files, covers how to compile Bicep templates to ARM templates before deployment, or if there is an existing ARM template, how to decompile it to a Bicep file.

Chapter 5, Defining Resources, explains how to define resources in a Bicep template, their properties, and dependencies, and some of the language specification that helps you to understand why Bicep is designed the way it is.

Chapter 6, Using Parameters, Variables, and Template Functions, takes you one step further to make your template customizable, remove duplicate expressions using variables, and use the template functions to create better, more reusable templates.

Chapter 7, Understanding Expressions, Symbolic Names, Conditions, and Loops, expands on the previous chapter to help you write template expressions, use logical flows and conditions, and use loops to create a resource multiple times without repeating the syntax.

Chapter 8, Defining Modules and Utilizing Outputs, introduces modules and helps you create modular, reusable templates that not only can be consumed by your own templates but also other teams within your organization. It also reviews template outputs and how to send information about the deployment outside of your templates.

Chapter 9, Deploying a Local Template, starts the process of validating and deploying your templates. Before you start using your templates in your CI/CD pipelines, you need to know how to test and deploy them locally, and that is what you will learn here.

Chapter 10, Deploying Bicep Using Azure DevOps, helps you set up an Azure pipeline to deploy your Azure resources from Azure Repos. It covers not only the creation of the pipeline but also how to add the necessary steps to validate and deploy a Bicep template.

Chapter 11, Deploying Bicep Templates Using GitHub Actions, helps you validate and deploy your Bicep templates from GitHub using a GitHub Actions workflow.

Chapter 12, Exploring Best Practices for Future Maintenance, complements your learning by introducing you to some best practices that will take your Bicep template creation to the next level.

To get the most out of this book

To take full advantage of this book, you will need to have the following list of software installed on your system. You also need to have an Azure DevOps and a GitHub account. Finally, you need to have an active Azure subscription, which you can get for free, all of which is described in the book.

Software/hardware covered in the book	OS requirements
Azure CLI	Windows, macOS X, and Linux (any)
Azure PowerShell	Windows, macOS X, and Linux (any)
Visual Studio Code	Windows, macOS X, and Linux (any)
Git	Windows, macOS X, and Linux (any)

I highly recommend that you follow along with the book to get the best out of it. Also feel free to use other types of resources for your own benefit, and when in doubt, always refer to Microsoft's documentation on Bicep.

Download the example code files

You can download the example code files for this book from GitHub at `https://github.com/PacktPublishing/Infrastructure-as-Code-with-Azure-Bicep`. In case there's an update to the code, it will be updated on the existing GitHub repository.

We also have other code bundles from our rich catalog of books and videos available at `https://github.com/PacktPublishing/`.

Check them out!

Download the color images

We also provide a PDF file that has color images of the screenshots/diagrams used in this book. You can download it here: `https://static.packt-cdn.com/downloads/9781801813747_ColorImages.pdf`.

Conventions used

There are several text conventions used throughout this book.

`Code in text`: Indicates code words in the text, database table names, folder names, filenames, file extensions, pathnames, dummy URLs, user input, and Twitter handles. Here is an example: "If you want to upgrade your Bicep, you can use the `upgrade` command."

A block of code is set as follows:

```
resource stg 'Microsoft.Storage/storageAccounts@2021-02-01' = {
  name: 'name'
  location: resourceGroup().location
  kind: 'StorageV2'
  sku: {
    name: 'Standard_LRS'
  }
}
output storageKey string = stg.listKeys().key[0].value
```

Any command-line input or output is written as follows:

```
brew update && brew install azure-cli
```

Bold: Indicates a new term, an important word, or words that you see on screen. For example, words in menus or dialog boxes appear in the text like this. Here is an example: "You can find the complete schema for all Azure resources in the **Schema** section of the Azure documentation."

> **Tips or Important notes**
> Appear like this.

Get in touch

Feedback from our readers is always welcome.

General feedback: If you have questions about any aspect of this book, mention the book title in the subject of your message and email us at customercare@packtpub.com.

Errata: Although we have taken every care to ensure the accuracy of our content, mistakes do happen. If you have found a mistake in this book, we would be grateful if you would report this to us. Please visit www.packtpub.com/support/errata, selecting your book, clicking on the Errata Submission Form link, and entering the details.

Piracy: If you come across any illegal copies of our works in any form on the internet, we would be grateful if you would provide us with the location address or website name. Please contact us at copyright@packt.com with a link to the material.

If you are interested in becoming an author: If there is a topic that you have expertise in and you are interested in either writing or contributing to a book, please visit authors.packtpub.com.

Share Your Thoughts

Once you've read *Infrastructure as Code with Azure Bicep*, we'd love to hear your thoughts! Please click here to go straight to the Amazon review page for this book and share your feedback.

Your review is important to us and the tech community and will help us make sure we're delivering excellent quality content.

Section 1: Getting Started with Azure Bicep

In this section, as well as an introduction to Bicep and getting started, you will also learn how to create your first template, compile Bicep files, and convert ARM templates to Bicep.

This part of the book comprises the following chapters:

- *Chapter 1, An Introduction to Azure Bicep*
- *Chapter 2, Installing Azure Bicep*
- *Chapter 3, Authoring Experience*
- *Chapter 4, Compiling and Decompiling Bicep Files*

1

An Introduction to Azure Bicep

In this chapter, you're going to learn what Azure Bicep is, and you'll get a quick bit of background on why it was created and what problems it is trying to solve. There will be a comparison with its predecessor, ARM templates, and at the end, you will learn about some of its limitations.

This chapter will give you insights into the reason why Microsoft went to all the trouble of creating Azure Bicep, even though there are already many different third-party tools out there with similar functionalities and feature sets. It is important to learn the reasoning to be able to learn the language without any bias and make practical use of its powerful features.

In this chapter, we are going to cover the following main topics:

- What is Azure Bicep?
- Why was it created?
- How does it work?

Technical requirements

To make the most of this chapter, you will need to have a basic understanding of **Infrastructure as Code** (**IaC**), Azure ARM templates, and the Azure CLI. The code used throughout this chapter is stored in this GitHub repository: `https://github.com/PacktPublishing/Infrastructure-as-Code-with-Azure-Bicep/tree/main/Chapter01`.

What is Azure Bicep?

In this section, you will learn Azure Bicep and what it offers to developers and DevOps teams. There will be a few code snippets to get your eyes familiar with the syntax and, finally, an overview of its components and building blocks. But before we begin, let's review some concepts to make sure we are on the same page.

IaC

Currently, many companies try to automate their infrastructure creation and maintenance. To do that, and to further keep track of what is happening or has happened in their environments, they use a set of scripts or code files alongside tools and processes that streamline the whole deployment for them.

This practice is called IaC and helps every team to safely establish and configure the required infrastructure for their applications and solutions. This practice became even more simplified when all cloud providers added the ability for their customers to use it, which in terms of Microsoft is called **Azure Resource Manager** (**ARM**) templates.

ARM templates

Microsoft Azure used to have a deployment model called classic, which helped users deal with individual services (called cloud services) using three components: **service definition**, **service configuration**, and **service package**. There is no need to delve into the details of these concepts; suffice to say that soon they realized this approach needed to change if they wanted to allow their users to leverage the full potential of IaC.

That is when ARM was introduced as a new way of deploying cloud services in Azure that supported other tools, such as the Azure portal, the Azure CLI, Azure PowerShell, and all their SDKs. Here is what the new deployment model looks like:

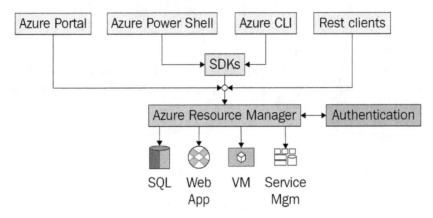

Figure 1.1 – Azure Resource Manager

As you can see, it's a much better-unified model, which allows their customers to deploy their resources using a centralized management layer. In addition to that, Microsoft introduced ARM templates, **JavaScript Object Notation (JSON)** documents, which would declare what resources are needed to be deployed and what the resource manager will use to deploy them in a group, along with their configuration and other files if needed.

Using ARM templates, developers and DevOps engineers can create repeatable deployments that offer auditability, extensibility, testing, modularity, previews, detailed logs, and a status update on the deployments as resources are getting created or modified.

Azure Bicep

Even though ARM templates are great to begin with, it turns out that JSON is not the ideal format to use, especially when the number of resources is high or the deployment model gets complex with time. So, Microsoft started to work on a project called Bicep as a revision to ARM templates to overcome some of the issues people were facing.

Azure Bicep is a **Domain-Specific Language** (**DSL**) that has all the benefits of ARM templates, but instead of using JSON, it uses a new language to overcome its shortcomings. It is designed to simplify the authoring experience of IaC and bring more integration with other tools, such as the Azure CLI and Visual Studio Code.

It is worth mentioning that Azure Bicep files will get transpiled to ARM templates very much like how TypeScript files transpile to JavaScript. This means every type, resource, and property that is valid in an ARM template is valid in Bicep as well. We will not go into the details of what a Bicep file looks like, but to pique your curiosity, here is the famous `Hello World!` in Bicep language:

```
param message string
var hello = 'Hello World! - Hi'
output helloWorld string = '${hello} ${message}'
```

When you compile this file, you will get an ARM template that looks like the following:

```json
{
    „$schema": „https://schema.management.azure.com/
schemas/2019-04-01/deploymentTemplate.json#",
    "contentVersion": "1.0.0.0",
    "metadata": {
      "_generator": {
        "name": "bicep",
        "version": "dev",
        "templateHash": "14991011523779832704"
      }
    },
    "parameters": {
      "message": {
        "type": "string"
      }
    },
    "functions": [],
    "variables": {
      "hello": "Hello World! - Hi"
    },
    "resources": [],
```

```
    "outputs": {
      "helloWorld": {
        "type": "string",
        "value": "[format('{0} {1}', variables('hello'),
  parameters('message'))]"
      }
    }
  }
```

It is amazing how simplified the Bicep file is, don't you agree? Some of the advantages of Azure Bicep are as follows:

- Support for all current resource providers
- A syntax that simplifies the IaC and can reduce a huge amount of code compared to ARM templates
- No need to manage any state (compared to some third-party tools, such as Terraform)
- Native integration with Microsoft tools, such as the Azure CLI and Visual Studio Code
- A modular structure that allows you to break your code and create your IaC with peace of mind
- Backed up by Microsoft support plans
- Native integration with other Azure resources, such as Azure Policy and Blueprints

Why was it created?

Now is the time to delve into why Microsoft felt there was a need to create another revision on ARM templates, which will be covered in this section. In addition, we will have a look at the rationale behind when to use third-party tools such as Pulumi or Terraform, and when to go with Bicep.

Why create a new revision?

ARM templates had some issues that were causing many customers to complain about the usage of JSON and its limitations. The first thing that was causing some pain was the way validation worked in ARM templates. Often, the template validation passed but the deployment would fail.

Another reason was not having to comment in the template, especially if the deployment model was very complex. I am not a fan of commenting in code or any script for that matter, but the lack of commenting, even small comments to deliver a hint to the next maintainer or team member, was not something people were happy about.

And the last valid reason was how parameters would be duplicated for different resources or environments. Given the fact that ARM templates themselves are reusable, this was not ideal and would make maintaining the parameter files a nightmare, although they might contain the same value.

To overcome these issues, Microsoft started to investigate different existing tools and new ways to enhance the functionality of ARM templates and, in the end, they ended up with the Bicep language, with its own syntax.

They mentioned in their GitHub repository that they went through more than 120 customer calls and surveyed their **Most Valuable Professionals (MVPs)** network, and evaluated and even prototyped a version written in TypeScript, but eventually decided that Bicep should have its own syntax.

And to me, it is a valid reason, since the majority of companies will use DevOps engineers or even cloud enablement teams to implement and maintain the IaC. Many of those people do not have familiarity with programming languages, which means that using a high-level language would incur a learning curve many companies cannot afford. On the other hand, many of those folks know scripting languages and can learn Bicep really fast without too much effort.

What about current third-party tools?

Another question people usually ask is why they can't use current tools, such as Pulumi or Terraform. For Pulumi, I have already explained the barrier of knowing a required programming language and the learning curve that would follow. For those who are comfortable using Terraform or are already using it, there would not be any reason to shift to Bicep at all. Of course, that is whether you are happy to pay the price to use Terraform Cloud when Bicep is a free tool.

In fact, Microsoft has already invested in creating a set of documentation to streamline the learning material in their DevOps site regarding using Terraform on Azure, which can be found at `https://azure.microsoft.com/en-au/solutions/devops/terraform`.

That said, many organizations – some of which I personally have worked with – are using ARM templates and are looking for a solution with the least overhead to move on. For those people, Bicep works well because they are already familiar with concepts such as built-in functions, types, API versions, and so on.

Furthermore, for those who have not started their journey in IaC, it would be much easier to start with something that has integration with the tools they would use, such as the Azure CLI and Visual Studio Code, with as little learning as possible, keeping in mind that Bicep is now supported by Microsoft support plans.

How does it work?

Now that you know what Bicep is and why it was created, it is time to learn how it works and what it takes to get started with it, which you will learn in this section.

Authoring experience

You can create and use Bicep files with Visual Studio Code using the official Bicep Visual Studio Code extension, which can be found at `https://github.com/Azure/bicep/blob/main/docs/installing.md#bicep-vs-code-extension`.

Figure 1.2 – Visual Studio Code Bicep extension

This means it really feels like a native experience, with all the bells and whistles of autocorrection, IntelliSense, validation warnings, and so on.

To make it even more exciting, both the Azure CLI and Azure PowerShell have built-in support for Bicep. That means you can compile and deploy a Bicep file just like you were doing with ARM templates. The transpilation happens behind the scenes for you and deployment will run afterward.

To give you an example, with ARM templates you use the `az deployment group create` command to start a new deployment, like so:

```
az group deployment create \
 -g myResourceGroup -n myDeployment \
 --template-file ./deploy.json \
 --parameters ./deploy.parameters.json \
 --parameters "sqlSAPassword=$password"
```

The procedure with Bicep would look very similar, if not identical, since the Azure CLI and PowerShell already support Bicep files as templates:

```
az deployment group create \
 -g myResourceGroup -n myDeployment \
 --template-file ./main.bicep \
 --parameters @parameters.json
```

And you should have your template deployed shortly after the command is successful. This is great, since you can easily use your Bicep files rather than compiling them first and then deploying them using one of these scripting tools, which adds extra time to your deployments and potentially adds unnecessary complexity to your pipeline steps.

What happens to my ARM templates?

If you already have ARM templates you wish to migrate to Bicep, the easiest solution is to use its CLI to decompile your JSON files by running the following command:

```
az bicep decompile --file azuredeploy.json
```

We will delve into this in much more detail in our upcoming chapters, but I just wanted to let you know in advance that there is no need to worry about the migration of your ARM templates into Bicep. In fact, since even the deployment commands are the same, there would be minimal changes required to your pipeline scripts.

> **Warning**
> As with any other tool, decompilation might result in a scenario where it would result in warnings or errors, which should be resolved by you. The possibility is not that high, but it might happen. One of the reasons might be that you are using copy loops or nested templates.

Bicep CLI

Bicep comes with its own *cross-platform* CLI, which will then be used by the Azure CLI and Azure PowerShell behind the scenes to compile/decompile Bicep/ARM template files. We will talk about this in much more detail later.

For example, if you wanted to decompile an ARM template to Bicep as we saw before, you would use a script like so:

```
bicep decompile --file azuredeploy.json
```

We will review this feature in much more detail later in the book.

Summary

In this chapter, we had a lot to discuss, a few concepts to agree on, and a few comparisons to make. You learned what IaC is very briefly, and then I made sure you knew about ARM templates, since that is the whole reason Bicep was created.

That was then followed by what Azure Bicep is, and you learned that it is not a new programming language and is a revision of ARM templates, with its own syntax. You saw why there was a need for creating yet another solution to implement IaC, even though there are plenty of tools, such as Pulumi and Terraform, out there. We talked about the cloud enablers not knowing any programming languages and the learning curve that would be in place if they had to learn a high-level language to do their day-to-day jobs.

Once that was settled, you learned how Bicep works and got to know the tools that can be used to create, compile, and deploy your resources using Bicep. We saw the built-in integration with the Azure CLI and Azure PowerShell, and how Bicep has its own CLI, which makes it easy for you to even decompile an ARM template into a Bicep file.

In the next chapter, we will get started with Bicep by going through how to install it on multiple different platforms.

2

Installing Azure Bicep

In this chapter, you are going to learn how to install Azure Bicep. Cross-platform installation tips using the Azure CLI or PowerShell Core and installation on each of the major operating systems are going to be covered.

At the end, you will learn how to install nightly builds if you are up for it and want to stay ahead of the curve.

In this chapter, we are going to cover the following main topics, but you can skip to the relevant section based on your platform of choice right away:

- Cross-platform installation
- Installation on Windows
- Manual installation on macOS
- Manual installation on Linux
- Getting nightly builds
- Working with Bicep in a Docker container

Technical requirements

To take full advantage of this chapter, you will need to have access to a personal computer or laptop that has Visual Studio Code and PowerShell Core installed. The code used throughout this chapter is stored in this GitHub repository at `https://github.com/PacktPublishing/Infrastructure-as-Code-with-Azure-Bicep/tree/main/Chapter02`.

Cross-platform installation

In this section, you will learn how to leverage the Azure CLI and Azure PowerShell to install Bicep cross-platform. This will include installing the **Azure CLI** and **Azure PowerShell** on **Windows**, **macOS**, and **Linux**.

Installing the Azure CLI

This approach is by far the easiest and the most convenient of all the possible ways to install Bicep. You will need to install the latest version of the Azure CLI or at least version 2.20.0 or above.

Installing the Azure CLI on Windows

To install the Azure CLI on Windows, you can either download the installer from `https://aka.ms/installazurecliwindows` or use the following command in a PowerShell window (PowerShell must be run as an administrator):

```
Invoke-WebRequest -Uri https://aka.ms/installazurecliwindows
-OutFile .\AzureCLI.msi; Start-Process msiexec.exe -Wait
-ArgumentList '/I AzureCLI.msi /quiet'; rm .\AzureCLI.msi
```

The following is the Azure CLI installation wizard window:

Figure 2.1 – Azure CLI installation wizard

If you already have it installed with a version lower than 2.20.0, you can run the upgrade command to get the latest version:

```
az upgrade
```

You can find out what version of the Azure CLI you have installed using the `az - version` command.

> **Note**
>
> The `az upgrade` command was added in version 2.11.0, so if your current version is below that, you need to uninstall it and install the latest version.

Installing the Azure CLI on Linux

To install the Azure CLI on Linux, you will need to refer to the official documentation site at `https://docs.microsoft.com/en-us/cli/azure/install-azure-cli-linux` since each distribution will use a different command. But for Debian/Ubuntu, the following command will suffice:

```
curl -sL https://aka.ms/InstallAzureCLIDeb | sudo bash
```

Installing the Azure CLI on macOS

On macOS, you can use Homebrew to install the Azure CLI and keep it updated. It has been tested with macOS version 10.9 and later and again, it is the most convenient approach among others. Simply run the following command to get it installed in no time:

```
brew update && brew install azure-cli
```

If you do not have Homebrew installed, feel free to install it from `https://docs.brew.sh/Installation.html`.

Installing Bicep using the Azure CLI

Once you have installed the Azure CLI, you are ready to move on to the next step, which is installing Bicep itself. Just run the `install` command and you should be good to go given you have the right version of the Azure CLI:

```
az bicep install
```

If you wanted to upgrade your Bicep, you can use the `upgrade` command:

```
az bicep upgrade
```

You now have everything you need to create and compile Bicep files and deploy them.

> **Note**
>
> When you install Bicep using the Azure CLI, it will be an independent version and would not conflict with any other versions you might have installed separately. The Bicep version can be checked using the `az bicep version` command.

Installing Bicep using Azure PowerShell

At the time of writing this book, Azure PowerShell does not install Bicep automatically like the Azure CLI does. However, you can install it manually and then use Azure PowerShell commands to deploy your Bicep files. We will cover manual installation on each platform shortly, but you need to be aware that you will need Azure PowerShell version 5.6.0 or above to be able to deploy Bicep files using Azure PowerShell. The version of Azure PowerShell can be checked using the following command:

```
Get-Module -ListAvailable -Name Azure -Refresh
```

If you do not have Azure PowerShell installed, refer to `https://docs.microsoft.com/en-us/powershell/azure/install-az-ps` and follow the instructions. If you have installed the Bicep CLI and have made sure you have Azure PowerShell installed, you should be good to deploy your Bicep files using the normal deployment commands:

```
New-AzResourceGroupDeployment -ResourceGroupName <resource-
group-name> -TemplateFile <path-to-bicep>
```

Once the command is executed, you would have the resources deployed in your Azure subscription.

Installation on Windows

To install the Bicep CLI on Windows, you have a few options. You can either use **Windows Installer**, **Chocolatey**, or **winget** or manually use PowerShell.

Installation using Windows Installer

You can download the installer from the following URL and install it: `https://github.com/Azure/bicep/releases/latest/download/bicep-setup-win-x64.exe`.

The following is the Azure Bicep CLI installation wizard:

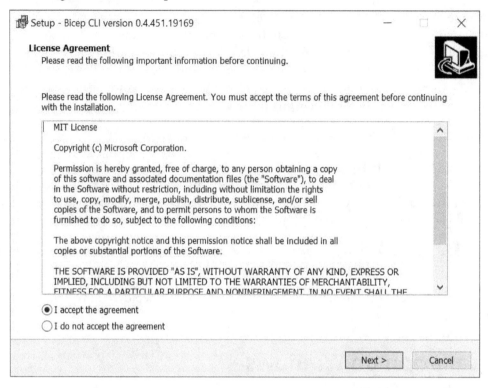

Figure 2.2 – Azure Bicep CLI wizard

You do not need to have administrator rights to do so and the CLI automatically gets added to your PATH environment variable for easy access from any terminal, whether it is the Windows terminal, the PowerShell window, or a WSL terminal.

Installation using Chocolatey

Chocolatey is a fantastic package manager for Windows that allows you to install your desired software using scripts instead of Windows installers, which is ideal for automation; think NuGet but for software. If you do not have it installed, head over to https://chocolatey.org/ and get it installed. Once done, simply run the following command to install the Bicep CLI:

```
choco install bicep
```

Like the Windows Installer, Chocolatey adds the necessary directory to your PATH environment variable, which means once done, you are ready to use the Bicep CLI in any terminal.

Installation using winget

winget is Microsoft's package manager and has similar functionalities to Chocolatey. You can discover, search for, install, upgrade, and remove applications to and from your Windows. However, you can only use it with computers with Windows 10 or above. **winget** has been added to Windows 10 or 11 Store for convenience, which is great since it can be updated using Windows Update. **winget** is included in the flight or preview version of Windows App Installer, which you can download and install from Windows Store, as shown in the following figure:

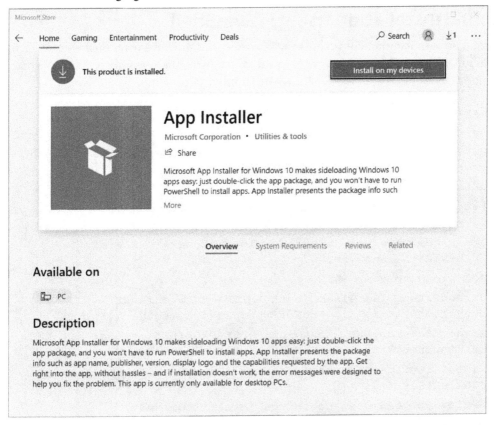

Figure 2.3 – winget installer from Microsoft Store on Windows

You can find out more about Winget and its features on its home page at https://docs.microsoft.com/en-us/windows/package-manager/winget/.

Once installed, run the installation command to get the Bicep CLI installed:

```
winget install -e --id Microsoft.Bicep
```

> **Note**
>
> winget is not a replacement for Chocolatey. It lacks features such as installing software using PowerShell scripts, installing Python packages, and deploying anything other than software such as license keys and files, to name a few. In general, it can only install MSI, MSIX, and some EXE files.

Manual installation using PowerShell

You can also install it manually using a set of commands in your PowerShell window. This will be suitable if you have other scripts to run or are using these as part of Azure Virtual Machine extensions or even the Desired State Configuration setup:

```powershell
# Create the install folder
$installPath = "$env:USERPROFILE\.bicep"
$installDir = New-Item -ItemType Directory -Path $installPath -Force
$installDir.Attributes += 'Hidden'
# Fetch the latest Bicep CLI binary
(New-Object Net.WebClient).DownloadFile("https://github.com/Azure/bicep/releases/latest/download/bicep-win-x64.exe", "$installPath\bicep.exe")
# Add bicep to your PATH
$currentPath = (Get-Item -path "HKCU:\Environment").GetValue('Path', '', 'DoNotExpandEnvironmentNames')
if (-not $currentPath.Contains("%USERPROFILE%\.bicep")) { setx PATH ($currentPath + ";%USERPROFILE%\.bicep") }
if (-not $env:path.Contains($installPath)) { $env:path += ";$installPath" }
# Verify you can now access the 'bicep' command.
bicep --help
# Done!
```

Once these commands are executed, you will have the CLI available and you're ready to get started.

Manual installation on macOS

If you want to install the Bicep CLI on macOS, you can use Homebrew, as you saw before, or via Bash scripts.

Installing Bicep via Homebrew

To install the Bicep CLI using Homebrew, simply run the following commands:

```
# Add the tap for bicep
brew tap azure/bicep
# Install the tool
brew install bicep
```

If you face any issues during installation, you can refer to the common issues on their GitHub repository at `https://github.com/Azure/azure-cli/issues`.

Installing Bicep via Bash

Finally, to install the Bicep CLI on macOS using Bash, you can use the following script:

```
# Fetch the latest Bicep CLI binary
curl -Lo bicep https://github.com/Azure/bicep/releases/latest/
download/bicep-osx-x64
# Mark it as executable
chmod +x ./bicep
# Add Gatekeeper exception (requires admin)
sudo spctl --add ./bicep
# Add bicep to your PATH (requires admin)
sudo mv ./bicep /usr/local/bin/bicep
# Verify you can now access the 'bicep' command
bicep --help
# Done!
```

Once done, you can start using the CLI right away.

Manual installation on Linux

Installing the Bicep CLI on Linux is a bit simpler. For regular distributions, use the following script to get it installed:

```
# Fetch the latest Bicep CLI binary
curl -Lo bicep https://github.com/Azure/bicep/releases/latest/
download/bicep-linux-x64
# Mark it as executable
chmod +x ./bicep
# Add bicep to your PATH (requires admin)
sudo mv ./bicep /usr/local/bin/bicep
# Verify you can now access the 'bicep' command
bicep --help
# Done!
```

However, if you have a lightweight distribution such as Alpine, use `bicep-linux-musl-x64` instead of `bicep-linux-x64` in the preceding script.

Getting nightly builds

If you would like to stay ahead of others and take advantage of new features, you can use the latest pre-release version of Bicep. Currently, the team will not publish the pre-release versions, so you need to go into their GitHub Actions run history and manually download the pre-release version you are after for the **main** branch.

Follow `https://github.com/Azure/bicep/actions` to view the latest action workflow. Once there, select the latest build that has been successful, as shown in the following screenshot:

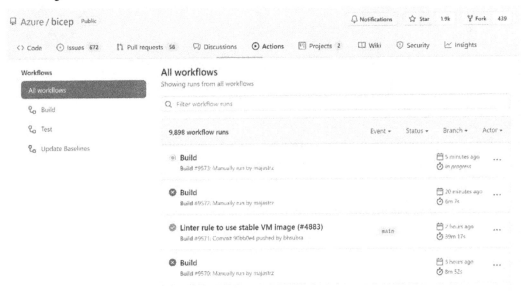

Figure 2.4 – Bicep's GitHub Action run history

On the build page, select the artifact you would like to download and install it according to one of the approaches we have gone through based on your operating system.

Artifacts
Produced during runtime

Name	Size
Bicep.LangServer	18.7 MB
Bicep.TestResults.linux-musl-x64	8.55 MB
Bicep.TestResults.linux-x64	8.55 MB
Bicep.TestResults.osx-x64	9.27 MB
Bicep.TestResults.win-x64	8.5 MB
bicep-nupkg-any	28.7 KB
bicep-nupkg-linux-x64	18.2 MB
bicep-nupkg-osx-x64	18.4 MB
bicep-nupkg-win-x64	18.3 MB
bicep-release-linux-musl-x64	40.4 MB
bicep-release-linux-x64	40.6 MB
bicep-release-osx-x64	41.3 MB
bicep-release-win-x64	39.3 MB
bicep-setup-win-x64	15.7 MB
playground	80.5 MB
vscode-bicep.vsix	23 MB

Figure 2.5 – Artifact list on nightly builds

> **Warning**
>
> These versions might have known or unknown issues much like any other beta or pre-release version of any software, so be mindful of that. Additionally, I would not recommend using these versions in any production environments unless vigorously tested.

Working with Bicep in a Docker container

We have covered many ways in which you can install Azure Bicep and get started. However, sometimes you do not wish to install it locally, or you simply want to leverage a Docker container to work with your Bicep files. In this section, we will cover how to do that.

Working with an Azure CLI Docker container

Fortunately, the Azure CLI has a Docker image that you can pull and use. Run the following commands to get the image and run it locally:

```
#pull the image
docker pull mcr.microsoft.com/azure-cli
#run the container
docker run -it --rm mcr.microsoft.com/azure-cli
#install bicep
az bicep install
#run the deployment using Azure CLI
az deployment group create -f main.bicep -g my-rg
```

Currently, the Docker image does not have Bicep pre-installed, so you need to install it. But as you saw, the installation is effortless and from here on, you have a full working environment at your disposal. This approach is also a good candidate for your **continuous integration** (**CI**) or **continuous delivery** (**CD**) pipelines if you have a container-based pipeline in place.

Summary

In this chapter, you have seen many ways in which you can install Azure Bicep, from using integrated tools such as the Azure CLI and Azure PowerShell, to manually installing the Bicep CLI on Windows, macOS, and Linux. You have also been introduced to nightly builds if you want to stay ahead of others and get the advantage of new features and bus fixes that the team publishes every night. To finish off on a high note, we saw how you could use a Docker container to deploy Bicep files to your Azure environment.

In the next chapter, we will cover the authoring experience and what it feels like for developers when they want to write Bicep files, and then validate and deploy them from their local environment.

3
Authoring Experience

So far, we have reviewed what Azure Bicep is and how to install it, but now it is time to review the authoring experience of Bicep files. In this chapter, you will learn about tools and the developer experience that is provided by Bicep. We will start with our most favorite code editor, **Visual Studio Code** (**VS Code**), and the Bicep extension that supports Bicep's syntax. We will then follow up with the built-in linter, which helps you inspect your code, as well as surfacing any warnings or errors as you are writing your code. Finally, we will review the Bicep Playground, which is a great place to start if you just want to see what a Bicep file looks like or review the syntax.

In this chapter, we are going to cover the following main topics:

- Bicep extension for VS Code
- Configuring the Bicep linter
- Bicep Playground

Technical requirements

To take full advantage of this chapter, you will need to have access to a personal computer or laptop that has Visual Studio Code and either PowerShell Core or the Azure CLI installed. The code that will be used in this chapter is stored in this book's GitHub repository at `https://github.com/PacktPublishing/Infrastructure-as-Code-with-Azure-Bicep/tree/main/Chapter03`.

Bicep extension for Visual Studio Code

Creating Bicep files should be easy and that is why it is very important to set up your developer environment. In this section, we will cover the basics and help you get set up. First off, you will need to install **Visual Studio Code**, then the **Bicep** extension, and make sure everything is ready for you to start hacking.

Installing Visual Studio Code

VS Code is Microsoft's powerful text editor and has ticked many boxes for developers around the world. It has become the most popular text editor because of it being free and offering so many features. It is a cross-platform tool that is very easy to install and work with. It has built-in support for JavaScript, TypeScript, and Node.js, as well as a world of extensions for other languages such as C#, C++, Python, PHP, and more.

You can find the installation instructions at `https://code.visualstudio.com/`. On that page, you can find `.msi`/`.exe` installers for Windows, `.deb` or `.rpm` files for Linux, and a `.zip` file for macOS, which is universal:

Figure 3.1 – Visual Studio Code installation wizard

You can install VS Code for your use only, or the entire system in Windows, Linux, or macOS. Once installed, you can start customizing your settings (the old tabs versus spaces debate), installing your desired extensions, creating code snippets, or even creating an extension if you cannot find what you are looking for. I highly recommend that you check out some of the blog posts that provide tips and tricks to boost your efficiency while developing, such as `https://code.visualstudio.com/docs/getstarted/tips-and-tricks`.

Installing the Bicep extension

The Bicep extension can be installed in VS Code and gives you a great authoring experience, such as IntelliSense and validation warnings and errors. It will validate not only the content of the Bicep file, but also the return types of all expressions (such as functions, resources, parameters, and outputs).

Now that you have VS Code installed, it is time to install the Bicep extension. Simply click on the extension icon on the left-hand sidebar and search for Bicep in the list:

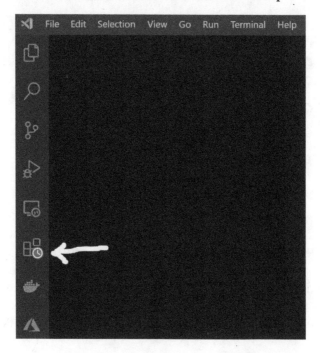

Figure 3.2 – Extension icon in VS code

Once found, click on **Install** to get the extension. If you have already installed the extension, you might see an **Uninstall** button instead:

Figure 3.3 – Finding and installing the Bicep extension in VS Code

Once the extension has been installed, you create a new Bicep file and check whether it is recognized by VS Code or not by looking at the bottom bar and seeing **Bicep** as the extension:

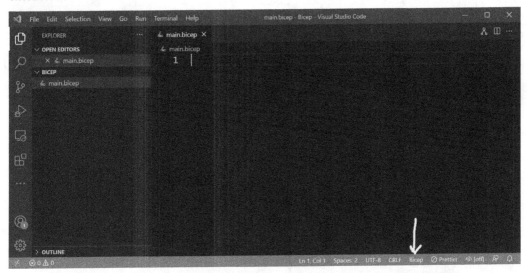

Figure 3.4 – VS Code recognizing the Bicep file and showing its extension type

> **Note**
> If you had the Bicep CLI v0.2 installed previously, you will need to uninstall that and install the new version. Otherwise, they will run side by side and you might get duplicated or inconsistent errors.

Snippets offered by the Bicep extension

The Bicep extension adds many value-added features beyond validation and IntelliSense. For example, you will have code snippets you can use to quickly populate a resource in your Bicep file. Let's try and use one of these snippets and see the results. In your newly created Bicep file, type `res-stor`:

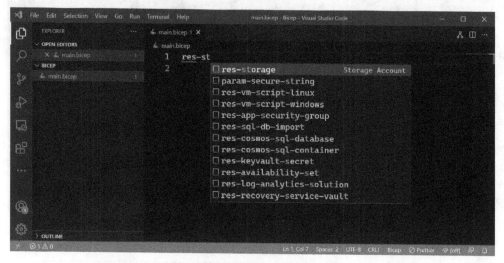

Figure 3.5 – Code snippets for Bicep provided by the extension

Once you see `res-storage`, press the *Enter* or *Tab* key. The full resource will be populated for you in your file:

```
1  resource storageaccount 'Microsoft.Storage/storageAccounts@2021-02-01' = {
2    name: 'name'
3    location: resourceGroup().location
4    kind: 'StorageV2'
5    sku: {
6      name: 'Premium_LRS'
7    }
8  }
9
10
```

Figure 3.6 – The full resource populated by the Bicep extension's code snippets

Here, you can see that some default values have been provided for the properties, but that is where you can start customizing and getting them from parameters, which we will cover later in this book.

Refactoring

You can easily rename symbols such as `param`, `resource`, or `format` in your Bicep files because of the extension. To rename a symbol, right-click on the symbol and select **Rename Symbol** (or press *F2*). I have extracted the name of our storage resource into a parameter to demonstrate this feature. I can highlight the parameter by clicking or putting the mouse cursor on it:

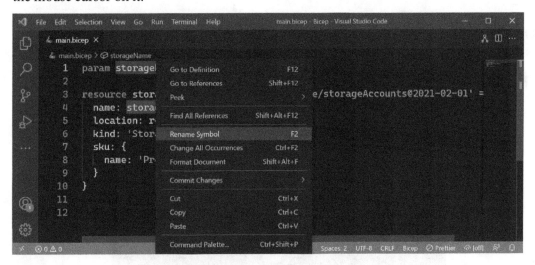

Figure 3.7 – Rename Symbol menu in VS Code

Now, type in your new name and press *Enter*. You should see that all the references with the same symbol have been renamed to your new value:

```
param storageName string

resource storageaccount 'Microsoft.Storage/storageAccounts@2021-02-01' = {
  name: storageName
  location: resourceGroup().location
  kind: 'StorageV2'
  sku: {
    name: 'Premium_LRS'
  }
}
```

Figure 3.8 – Symbol renamed everywhere in the Bicep file

Formatting

Formatting is as easy as right-clicking and selecting the format option. Beware that sometimes, you might have other formatters that prevent you from using the Bicep extension, such as the global formatter. You can find this by going into your settings (*Ctrl + ,*) and switching to the JSON version by clicking on the 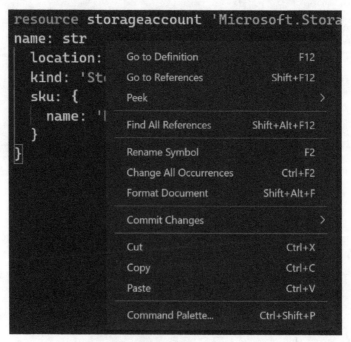 icon. You can add the following code snippet to the end of the file to make sure your Bicep files are picked up by the right formatter:

```
"[bicep]": {
        "editor.defaultFormatter": "ms-azuretools.vscode-bicep"
    }
```

Once you have this, you are good to start formatting your files. The shortcut for Windows is *Shift + Alt + F*:

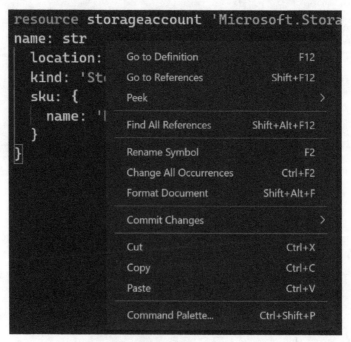

Figure 3.9 – Formatting a Bicep file in VS Code

Using quick fixes

Sometimes, you will be typing quickly and make a mistake, which might cause a warning or error line underneath the symbol you just typed. Simply hover your mouse over the item, then click on the blue light bulb icon and select **Quick Fix**. The Bicep extension will do its best to fix the problem. This works for many scenarios but like in the previous examples, you cannot expect it to work for everything:

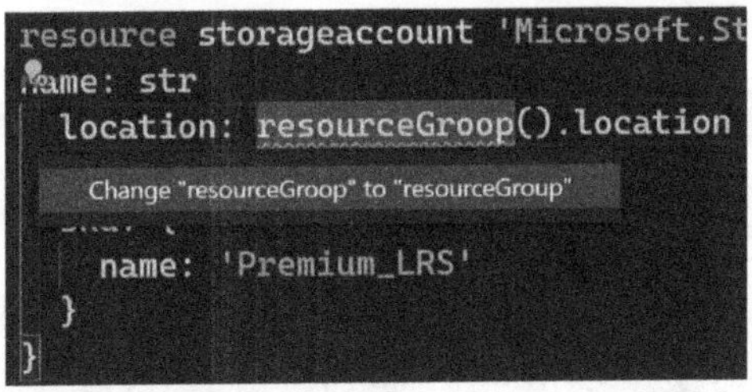

Figure 3.10 – Leveraging Quick Fix to rectify mistakes

Configuring the Bicep linter

The Bicep linter is the sugar on the top for your development environment setup. It can analyze your Bicep files and check for syntax errors and help you create better Bicep files that adhere to coding standards during development. You will need to have VS Code and the Bicep extension installed, in addition to the Bicep CLI. You should be now fully aware of how to install those tools. Once installed, you should be able to start customizing the linter rules.

Customizing the linter

You need to create a file called `bicepconfig.json` in the root of the folder you are working with to customize the rules controlled by the linter. In this file, you will supply rule-specific values that set the level of those rules and/or enable/disable them at the same time. Please note that you can have multiple nested folders and multiple config files within each of those, in which case the closest config file overrides the one located in the parent folder:

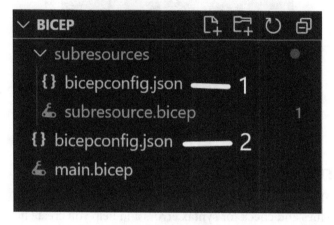

Figure 3.11 – Priority of the Bicep config files in nesting folders

Now that we know how these configuration files affect our linting rules, let's look at an example to understand how we can control these rules. For this example, let's assume that we would like to prevent a developer from hardcoding any environment URLs. We need to add the following code to our configuration file:

```
{
  "analyzers": {
    "core": {
      "verbose": false,
      "enabled": true,
      "rules": {
        "no-hardcoded-env-urls": {
          "level": "warning",
          "disallowedhosts": [
            "management.core.windows.net",
            "management.azure.com",
            "database.windows.net",
            "core.windows.net"
```

```
          ],
            "excludedhosts": [
              "schema.management.azure.com"
            ]
          }
        }
      }
    }
  }
```

First, you can see a property called `enable` that is set to `true`. If you set this to `false`, the linter will ignore any rules here.

You also have a `verbose` flag that is set to `false`. If you want more detailed information, including which config file is causing this error or warning, you can set this to `true`.

Next, pay attention to the `rules` section in the preceding code snippet. This is where all the customizations will be placed. Each rule is a key-value pair, with the key being a string and the value being either an object, number, Boolean, string, array, and so on. We are preventing anybody from using any URL that has those four domain names, except for the schema URL, since it might be used for validation or specifying a particular API version.

Here is a more complete example that contains more rules that can help you keep your Bicep files clean and more aligned with coding standards:

```
{
  "analyzers": {
    "core": {
      "enabled": true,
      "verbose": true,
      "rules": {
        "no-hardcoded-env-urls": {
          "level": "warning"
        },
        "no-unused-params": {
          "level": "error"
        },
        "no-unused-vars": {
          "level": "error"
```

```
    },
    "prefer-interpolation": {
      "level": "warning"
    },
    "secure-parameter-default": {
      "level": "error"
    },
    "simplify-interpolation": {
      "level": "warning"
    }
  }
 }
}
```

In the preceding example, we are specifying that we want to enforce the following rules:

- No hardcoded URLs with a warning level.
- No unused parameters with an error level.
- No unused variables with an error level.
- Preferring string interpolation over concatenation with a warning level.
- No default values are hardcoded for secure parameters with an error level.
- It is not necessary to use interpolation to reference a parameter or variable.

The `level` property can have four values:

- **Error**: Any violation of a rule with this level will cause an error that, in turn, prevents the build from being successful.
- **Warning**: Violating any rule with this level will show you a warning, but you can still build and deploy your Bicep file.
- **Info**: Violation of a rule with this level will not appear in the output, but you will see a squiggle line appear underneath the culprit line or symbol.
- **Off**: This will turn the rule completely off. Any warnings or errors will be suppressed under any rule with this level.

The Bicep extension also helps you with filling out these rules in your config files by showing you suggestions as you start typing using the IntelliSense feature:

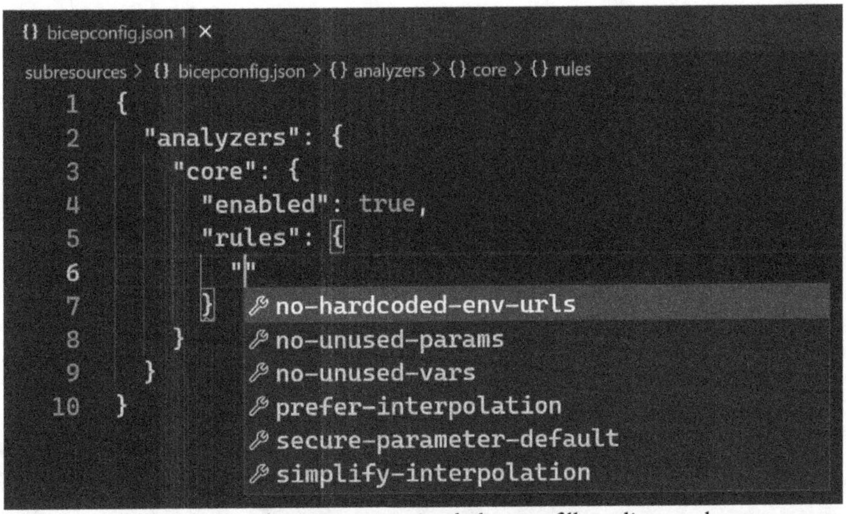

Figure 3.12 – The Bicep extension helps you fill out linter rules

If you wanted to see all the errors and warnings in one place, VS Code will help you by centralizing all of them in the **PROBLEMS** pane in the integrated terminal. Simply open the integrated terminal (*Ctrl + Shift + `*) and click on the **PROBLEMS** pane to see the full list:

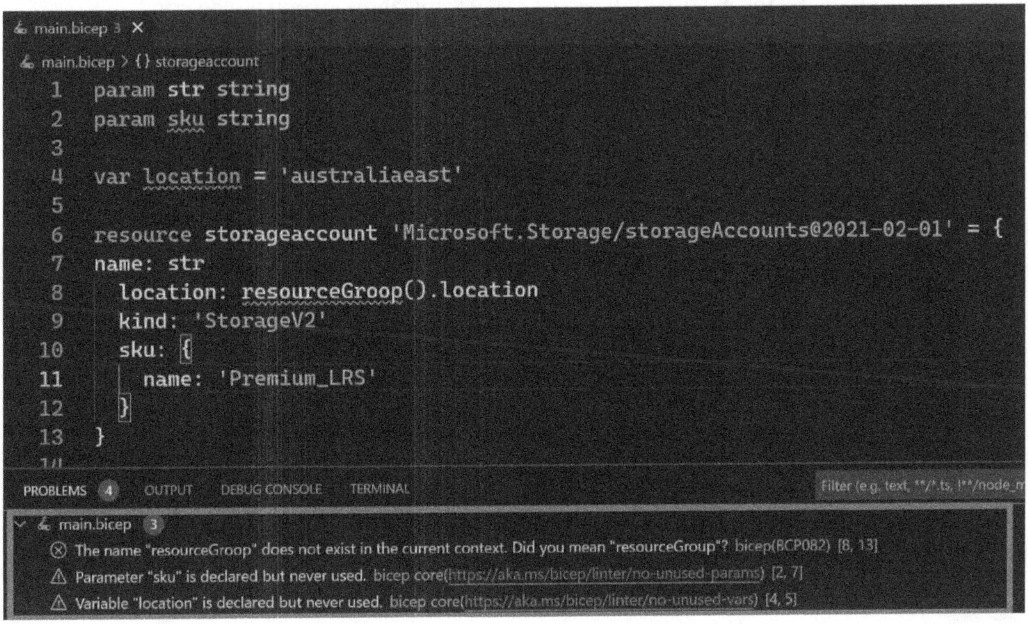

Figure 3.13 – Errors and warnings highlighted by the Bicep linter in VS Code

You can click on each of the blue links to find out more about each linting rule. At the end of each line, there is a line number you can use to pinpoint where the warning or error is occurring within your Bicep file.

Using the Bicep CLI to use the linter

You can also use the Bicep CLI to find out about any error or warning in your Bicep file. This could be useful if you wanted to use this approach in your continuous integration pipeline to catch anything before deploying your resources. Simply open a terminal or command prompt in your directory where your Bicep file is and run the `build` command:

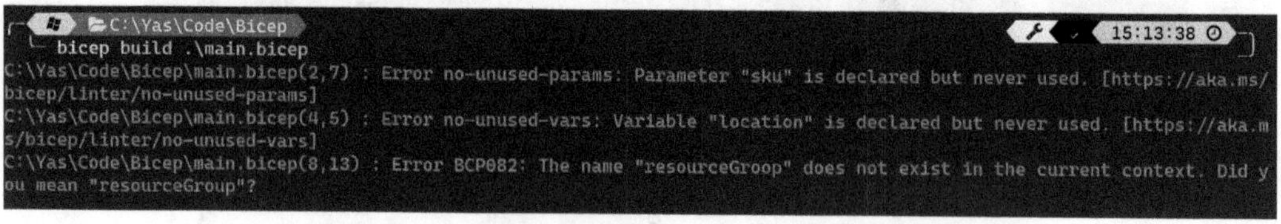

```
🗗 ➦C:\Yas\Code\Bicep                                                    🔧 ◢ 15:13:38 🕐
    bicep build .\main.bicep
C:\Yas\Code\Bicep\main.bicep(2,7) : Error no-unused-params: Parameter "sku" is declared but never used. [https://aka.ms/
bicep/linter/no-unused-params]
C:\Yas\Code\Bicep\main.bicep(4,5) : Error no-unused-vars: Variable "location" is declared but never used. [https://aka.m
s/bicep/linter/no-unused-vars]
C:\Yas\Code\Bicep\main.bicep(8,13) : Error BCP082: The name "resourceGroop" does not exist in the current context. Did y
ou mean "resourceGroup"?
```

Figure 3.14 – Using Bicep CLI v0.4.x to use the linter

> **Note**
>
> You can only use the linter with Bicep CLI v0.4.x and above. If you build your Bicep and cannot see any error, check your version using `bicep -v`.

If you do not have the correct version, you can manually upgrade your Bicep CLI or just run the `upgrade` command using the Azure CLI:

```
Az bicep upgrade
```

Once executed, you should see the upgraded version:

```
🗗 ➦C:\Yas\Code\Bicep
    bicep -v
Bicep CLI version 0.4.626 (be3afce39f)
```

Figure 3.15 – Getting the Bicep CLI version

As you can see, it is very simple to work and configure the Bicep linter to have a much more effective authoring experience and become aware of warnings and errors.

Bicep Playground

Azure Bicep Playground is a useful tool if you do not wish to install the tooling locally, but still want to review the syntax and have a go at verifying what would be the result of your Bicep file or what would be the equivalent of your ARM template in Bicep.

The tool is hosted at `https://bicepdemo.z22.web.core.windows.net/` and once loaded, it will contain an example Bicep file with multiple resources and its equivalent ARM template JSON object.

Compiling Bicep snippets

I recommend removing everything and simply pasting the storage object you had in the previous example into the Bicep section on the left-hand side. You should see the JSON being populated immediately:

Figure 3.16 – Compiling a Bicep file with Azure Bicep Playground

If you have any errors in your snippets, the tool will not generate the JSON and show you a compilation failure message:

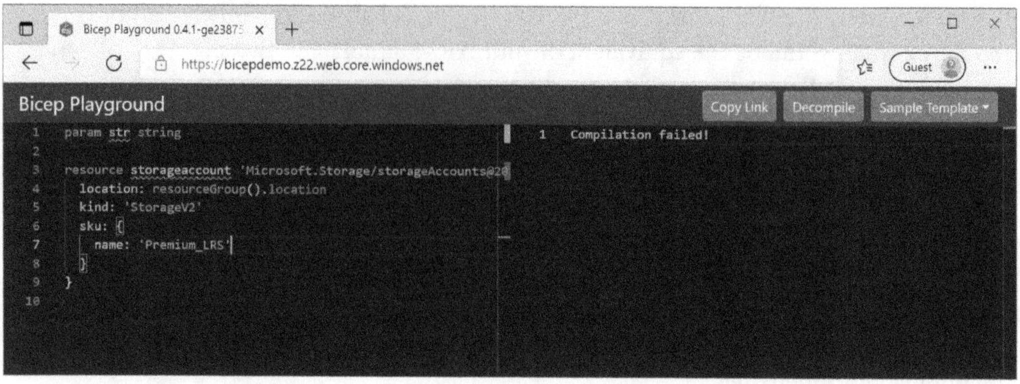

Figure 3.17 – Compilation error shown in the Bicep Playground for invalid Bicep files

This is a good way to get started without having to install any tools locally.

Decompiling an ARM template

You can also decompile your ARM templates using the playground, but instead of copying and pasting your code, you need to upload a JSON file into the tool by clicking on the **Decompile** button:

Figure 3.18 – Decompiling ARM templates into Bicep using Bicep Playground

If we use the output of our current Bicep file, we will see the decompiled version on the left-hand side panel immediately:

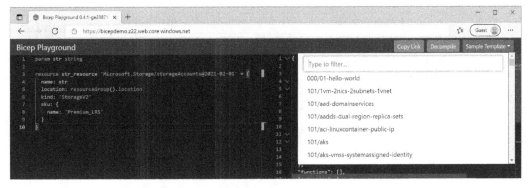

Figure 3.19 – Decompiled version of an ARM template in Bicep Playground

From here, you can simply copy the resulting Bicep code and use it in your environments. You can also decompile an ARM template using the Bicep CLI, which we will cover later in this book.

Using sample templates in Bicep Playground

There is another great functionality in Bicep Playground where you can use some sample templates that have been created by the community. There are many sample templates and a search box in case you wanted to search for a specific template:

Figure 3.20 – Using sample templates in Bicep Playground

Go ahead and type `storage`, then select the template named `101/storage-blob-container` to see the results.

Summary

In this chapter, we reviewed how to set up the Bicep extension in VS Code to create a powerful and efficient developer environment that helps you get started with Bicep using a rich authoring experience. Then, we saw how we can configure the Bicep linter to leverage its power and make the authoring experience even better by finding warnings and errors using the Bicep configuration files. You learned how to configure different rules with different levels and make sure your Bicep files are adhering to coding standards that are used by the developer community and other organizations.

You also got to know Azure Bicep Playground, which helps you compile your Bicep files into ARM templates, decompile your ARM templates to see the resulting Bicep file, and take advantage of hundreds of sample templates created by the community to become familiar with Bicep, without the need to install any tool on your local environment.

In the next chapter, we will cover compiling and decompiling Bicep/ARM templates in more detail.

4
Compiling and Decompiling Bicep Files

So far, you have learned what a Bicep file is, how to install it, and what the authoring experience looks like. Now, it is time to take a look at the different ways in which to compile your Bicep files or, on the other side of the equation, convert an existing ARM template into a Bicep file if you are migrating.

In this chapter, you will learn how to compile your Bicep files and deal with any potential warnings and errors. Additionally, you will learn how to decompile an ARM template into a Bicep file.

In this chapter, we are going to cover the following main topics:

- Compiling a Bicep file using the Bicep CLI
- Troubleshooting potential warnings and errors
- Decompiling an ARM template into Bicep

Technical requirements

To take full advantage of this chapter, you will need to have access to a personal computer or laptop that has **Visual Studio Code** (**VS Code**) and PowerShell Core installed. The code used throughout this chapter is stored in the GitHub repository at `https://github.com/PacktPublishing/Infrastructure-as-Code-with-Azure-Bicep/tree/main/Chapter04`.

Compiling Bicep files

In this section, you will learn how to compile your **Bicep** files. The simplest way in which to compile your Bicep file is by using the **Bicep CLI**. By now, you should have it installed and ready to use.

Compiling a Bicep file using the Bicep CLI

The Bicep CLI has a `build` command that compiles a Bicep file and produces an ARM template. Create a new empty file and rename it `main.bicep`. You can also use the following command in both Linux and macOS:

```
ECHO >> main.bicep
```

Following this, open a terminal where the file is located and run the following:

```
bicep build main.bicep
```

This will produce the following output inside a file called `main.json`:

```
{
    "$schema": "https://schema.management.azure.com/
schemas/2019-04-01/deploymentTemplate.json#",
    "contentVersion": "1.0.0.0",
    "metadata": {
      "_generator": {
        "name": "bicep",
        "version": "0.4.626.15038",
        "templateHash": "18256579389878767151"
      }
    },
```

```
    "functions": [],
    "resources": []
}
```

Note that there is a file in the GitHub repository of the project, within the `Chapter04` folder, if you wish to follow along using that. Here is my VS Code window, which shows the result of the compilation within the same folder:

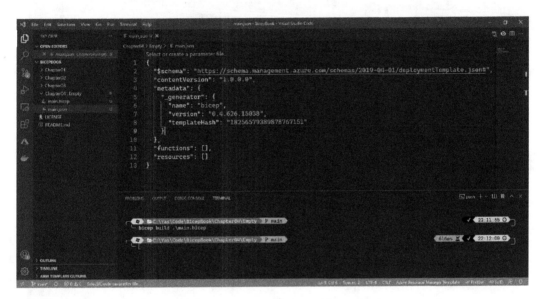

Figure 4.1 – Compiling an empty Bicep file

Now, it is time to compile a file containing a resource. So, let's go ahead and copy this code snippet into your Bicep file (you can also download the file from GitHub or clone the entire repository, linked to in the *Technical requirements* section):

```
resource storageaccount 'Microsoft.Storage/
storageAccounts@2021-02-01' = {
  name: 'name'
  location: resourceGroup().location
  kind: 'StorageV2'
  sku: {
    name: 'Standard_LRS'
  }
}
```

Now, run the `build` command again. This time, there should be an ARM template generated with a storage account inside the `resources` section:

```json
{
  "$schema": "https://schema.management.azure.com/
schemas/2019-04-01/deploymentTemplate.json#",
  "contentVersion": "1.0.0.0",
  "metadata": {
    "_generator": {
      "name": "bicep",
      "version": "0.4.626.15038",
      "templateHash": "7390125300479212842"
    }
  },
  "functions": [],
  "resources": [
    {
      "type": "Microsoft.Storage/storageAccounts",
      "apiVersion": "2021-02-01",
      "name": "name",
      "location": "[resourceGroup().location]",
      "kind": "StorageV2",
      "sku": {
        "name": "Standard_LRS"
      }
    }
  ]
}
```

Now you are ready to deploy the resulting template to Azure. However, note that this process will take some time and is not that efficient. So, let's review how to improve it.

Compiling and deploying a Bicep file using the Azure CLI

You can use the Azure CLI to build and deploy your Bicep files in one go rather than first compiling and then deploying afterward. The command is the same as the one you are used to using to deploy your ARM templates; however, instead of passing the JSON file, you pass the Bicep file. Let's go ahead and open a terminal in the same directory where you had your `main.bicep` file with the storage account inside.

Now run the following command:

```
az deployment group create '
    --template-file main.bicep '
    --resource-group myResourceGroup
```

The preceding command will compile your Bicep file, then deploy the content in the specified resource group. If you do not wish to deploy your template yet, read on to find out how it is possible.

The what-if deployment

Sometimes, you just want to see what would happen if you were to deploy your Bicep file but without actually deploying it. This is called a **dry-run** or **what-if** operation. When working with cloud environments, the Azure CLI and Azure PowerShell both support this operation. So, let's repeat the same step we just performed, but this time, we will use the `what-if` flag:

```
az deployment group what-if '
    --template-file main.bicep '
    --resource-group myResourceGroup
```

You should most likely see the following result:

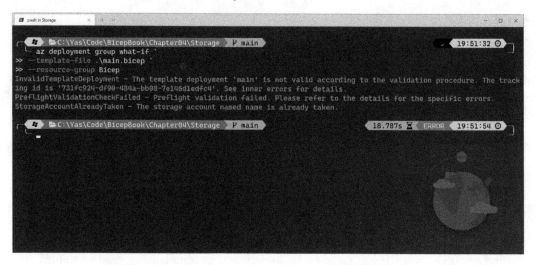

Figure 4.2 – Checking the Bicep files with a what-if operation

For a moment, let's forget the fact that there is an error. Interestingly, we have this validation without first having to deploy our resource into Azure. You could have received the same validation if your template was invalid or if there was another issue in your deployment, which is of great help to you and your team.

> **Note**
>
> To use what-if in the Azure CLI, you must have access to Azure CLI 2.14.0 or later.

The error was generated because the storage account name was not unique enough. So, let's go ahead and change the name to something a bit more unique or just use the following line instead:

```
'storage${uniqueString(resourceGroup().id)}'
```

Now run the command again. This time, you should be able to view the result of what would have happened if the template deployment was successful:

Figure 4.3 – The what-if deployment status

It is amazing to not only see that our Bicep file is valid but also that the deployment will be successful if we do go ahead with it.

Compiling and deploying a Bicep file using Azure PowerShell

Your experience will be the same even if you use Azure PowerShell instead of the Azure CLI. Simply run one of these commands based on your decision to deploy your template right away:

```
New-AzResourceGroupDeployment '
-ResourceGroupName Bicep '
-TemplateFile .\main.bicep
```

Or, just use the what-if operation:

```
New-AzResourceGroupDeployment -WhatIf '
-ResourceGroupName Bicep '
-TemplateFile .\main.bicep
```

> **Note**
>
> To use what-if in PowerShell, you must have version 4.2, or later, of the Az module.

Please note that I have used the backtick (') symbol to go to the next line in the terminal since I have used a PowerShell-based window. If you have Bash or any other Unix-based command prompt, you will need to replace it with a backslash (\) symbol.

You might end up with a warning or an error when compiling your Bicep files, and that is OK. In the following section, we will cover the steps that you need to follow to find out what is wrong and how to fix it quickly.

Troubleshooting possible errors and warnings

You might, and most probably will, face challenges when compiling or deploying your Bicep files, and it is important to understand where to look to find the issue. I will only cover errors relating to how to compile your Bicep files here. We will take a deeper look at many more errors in *Chapter 9, Deploying a Local Template*.

An invalid template

Sometimes, you might have an invalid template. This might be because you copied the snippets from elsewhere or even unintentionally caused it yourself:

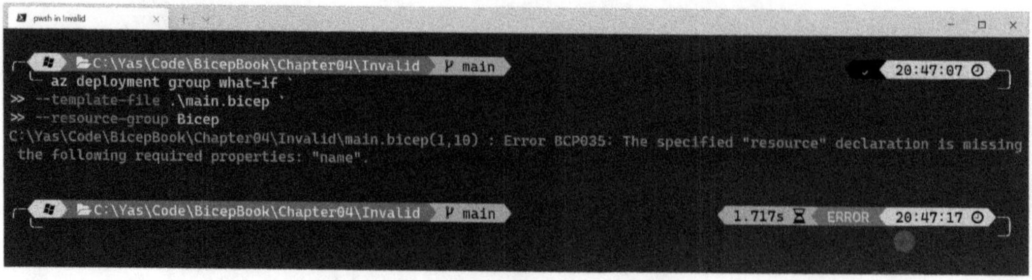

Figure 4.4 – Template validation errors

This is, by far, the simplest error to troubleshoot because the CLI tells you exactly what is wrong and where to look for it down to the line number. Simply go and fix the stated problem and try again.

Linter errors

If you are using linter files, you might face errors caused by your rules. You will need to fix them before deploying your Bicep file. The following screenshot shows an example of a template that has a syntax error:

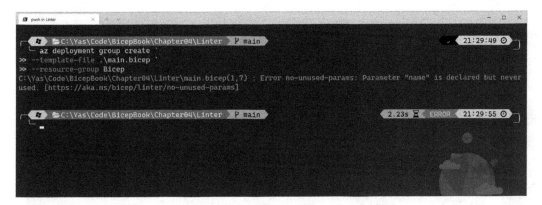

Figure 4.5 – Linter errors

Note that you will need to fix all of the linter errors before you can successfully compile or deploy your Bicep files. Generally, these errors are related to the syntax and validation rules enforced by you or your team.

The last thing we need to cover is how to decompile or convert an existing ARM template into a Bicep file if we are migrating to Bicep or simply getting started with Bicep but do not use any template for deployment. The following section will cover this particular scenario.

Decompiling ARM templates into Bicep

Now that you understand how to compile your Bicep files and can troubleshoot any possible errors or warnings, it is time to show you how to migrate your existing templates into Bicep. You have already seen the Azure Bicep Playground and its decompile option in *Chapter 3, Authoring Experience*, so I will not cover it again here. Instead, we will use the CLI to decompile an ARM template into Bicep.

All you need to do is use one of the following methods.

Using the Azure CLI

To use the Azure CLI to decompile an ARM template, simply run the following command:

```
az bicep decompile --file main.json
```

Once the command has been completed, you should see the resulting Bicep file in the same location:

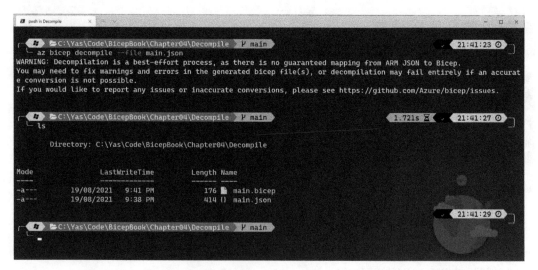

Figure 4.6 – Decompiling an ARM template into Bicep using the Azure CLI

Now you have the Bicep file generated with the same name, and you can use it for future cases.

Using the Bicep CLI

You can use the Bicep CLI directly if you wish, and you should get the same result. The command will be as follows:

```
bicep decompile .\main.json
```

Next, let's take a look at the fixes we might need to apply after the decompilation process.

Potential fixes after decompiling

As stated in the warning in the output of the `decompile` command, the conversion is a best-effort attempt. Sometimes, you need to apply fixes after migration. One of the most common ones is the naming convention. Let's suppose you have a template as follows:

```
{
  "$schema": "https://schema.management.azure.com/
schemas/2019-04-01/deploymentTemplate.json#",
  "contentVersion": "1.0.0.0",
  "variables": {
    "storageAccountName": "[concat('store',
uniquestring(resourceGroup().id))]"
  },
  "resources": [
    {
      "type": "Microsoft.Storage/storageAccounts",
      "apiVersion": "2021-02-01",
      "name": "[variables('storageAccountName')]",
      "location": "[resourceGroup().location]",
      "kind": "StorageV2",
      "sku": {
        "name": "Standard_LRS"
      }
    }
  ]
}
```

When you decompile this template, you will see a Bicep file containing the following:

```
var storageAccountName_var =
'store${uniqueString(resourceGroup().id)}'
resource storageAccountName 'Microsoft.Storage/
storageAccounts@2021-02-01' = {
  name: storageAccountName_var
  location: resourceGroup().location
  kind: 'StorageV2'
  sku: {
    name: 'Standard_LRS'
```

```
    }
}
```

Pay attention to the variable name. You might agree that the name is not something you would normally choose for your variables, that is, with an underscore and a `var` keyword at the end. So, this is one of the things you might want to check and fix after decompilation.

Exporting templates and decompiling

Even if you do not have the ARM template for your resources, you can still export it from your existing resources. You can mix the `export` command and then decompile to achieve the desired result:

```
az group export --name "your_resource_group_name" > main.json
az bicep decompile --file main.json
```

This will export the ARM template of all resources in your resource group and then decompile it to Bicep. Of course, expect to apply some changes to the names and references, as mentioned earlier.

Summary

In this chapter, you learned how to compile your Bicep files and deploy them to Azure. Additionally, you learned how to try it out before deployment using the `what-if` flag. Following this, you discovered how to resolve some of the warnings or errors that you might face during compilation. Finally, we covered how to decompile an existing ARM template into Bicep just in case you started migrating your existing templates or simply wanted to get started with the export and creation of your infrastructure as code from your existing environment in Azure.

We hope you have enjoyed the book so far and continue to read on. From our next chapter onward, we will be officially getting into the core concepts of Bicep and exploring details such as how to define resources, what types are, the language specification, and a comparison between ARM and Bicep.

Section 2: Azure Bicep Core Concepts

This section details all the constructs of Azure Bicep to help you create the necessary resources for your solutions.

This part of the book comprises the following chapters:

5
Defining Resources

Looking back, you have come a long way. Starting with the basics of installation, followed by the authoring experience and how to compile and decompile to and from ARM templates, we have covered a lot. But we have just scratched the surface.

In this chapter, we will learn about defining resources, including how to reference existing resources and scopes. Once you become familiar with those, we will look at the Bicep type system and the language specification. To reinforce what you have learned, we will finish by providing a short syntax comparison with the ARM template.

In this chapter, we are going to cover the following main topics:

- Resource definition
- Referencing existing resources
- Resource scopes
- Bicep language specification
- Bicep type system
- ARM and Bicep syntax comparison

Technical requirements

To take full advantage of this chapter, you will need to have access to a personal computer or laptop that has **Visual Studio Code** (**VS Code**) and PowerShell installed on it. The code for this chapter is stored in this book's GitHub repository at `https://github.com/PacktPublishing/Infrastructure-as-Code-with-Azure-Bicep/tree/main/Chapter05`.

Resource definition

Remember that **ARM templates** have resource arrays and that everything you want to deploy will be placed in there. In **Bicep**, you define your resources at the top level, which is just one of its benefits. Simplifying the writing process has been at the forefront of the product team from the get-go and we can see it everywhere.

Every resource should be declared with `resource`, a reserved keyword. After that, you will need to define a symbolic name for your resource. This name is not used anywhere except for within the Bicep file. One of its use cases would be to reference this resource later down the line or output one of its properties.

Next, you will need a resource type and the API version you are using for that type. The resource type points to the resource provider that **Azure Resource Manager** (**ARM**) should use to deploy your resource. For more information on resource providers, please visit the official documentation at `https://docs.microsoft.com/en-us/azure/azure-resource-manager/management/resource-providers-and-types`.

Going back to our example from the previous chapter, let's put everything into perspective:

```
resource stg 'Microsoft.Storage/storageAccounts@2019-06-01' = {
    ...
}
```

Here, you can see the `resource` keyword, which is reserved, followed by the symbolic name `stg`, which is then followed by the resource type and the API version.

> **Note**
>
> At the time of writing this book, Bicep does not support the API profiles that are supported by ARM templates. API profiles help with avoiding the need to specify which API version is needed for every resource in the template by defining it at the top level. More information can be found at `https://docs.microsoft.com/en-us/azure/azure-resource-manager/templates/syntax#template-format`.

Common properties

Every resource has a set of common properties such as name, location, tags, and
sub-properties. These will be placed at the top level within the object hierarchy. Here
is our resource with a hardcoded name:

```
resource stg 'Microsoft.Storage/storageAccounts@2019-06-01' = {
  name: 'myStorageAccount'
  ...
}
```

Like ARM templates, you can define the name as a variable if name should be created with
a formula such as a unique name. Alternatively, you can get the name from parameters,
which we will cover in the next chapter.

Adding location to our storage account, plus a few tags, will make our resource look
as follows:

```
resource stg 'Microsoft.Storage/storageAccounts@2019-06-01' = {
  name: 'myStorageAccount'
  location: 'eastus'
  tags: {
    'Environment': "Dev"
    'Project': 'Azure Bicep'
  }
}
```

Now that the common properties have been set, it is time to add the resource-specific
properties.

Resource-specific properties

Some properties belong to specific resources. For our storage account, these could be its sku
and kind, as well as sub-properties such as accessTier. Here is our completed resource:

```
resource stg 'Microsoft.Storage/storageAccounts@2021-02-01' = {
  name: 'myStorageAccount'
  location: 'eastus'
  kind: 'StorageV2'
  sku: {
    name: 'Premium_LRS'
```

```
    }
    properties: {
      accessTier: 'Hot'
    }
    tags: {
      'Environment': 'Dev'
      'Project': 'Azure Bicep'
    }
}
```

If you are using VS Code, you do not need to worry about finding the values for these properties as the autocomplete feature provided by the Bicep extension will show them.

Adding additional properties

Since every resource that is supported by ARM templates is supported by Bicep, you have the option to add all of them to your resource definition. For example, you could enable system-assigned managed identities, network rules, HTTPS-only traffic, and more:

```
resource stg 'Microsoft.Storage/storageAccounts@2021-02-01' = {
  name: 'myStorageAccount'
  location: 'eastus'
  kind: 'StorageV2'
  sku: {
    name: 'Premium_LRS'
  }
  properties: {
    accessTier: 'Hot'
    allowBlobPublicAccess: true
    supportsHttpsTrafficOnly: true
    networkAcls: {
      defaultAction: 'Deny'
      virtualNetworkRules: [
        {
          id: 'SUBNET ID'
          action: 'Allow'
        }
      ]
```

```
      }
  }
  tags: {
     'Environment': 'Dev'
     'Project': 'Azure Bicep'
  }
  identity: {
     type: 'SystemAssigned'
  }
}
```

You can find the complete schema for all the Azure resources in the **Schema** section of the Azure documentation at `https://docs.microsoft.com/en-us/azure/templates/`. But what if you wanted to reference an existing resource? We will cover this next.

Referencing existing resources

There are two scenarios where you would want to reference an existing resource. The first is when a resource has been defined in the same template, while the second is when a resource has already been deployed to Azure. First, let's cover the scenario of referencing a resource that is included in the same template.

Referencing a resource that is in the same file

Remember that you need a symbolic name for every resource that is included in your Bicep file. You can use this same symbol so that you can use that resource later in your template. This might be required for a wide variety of reasons, such as accessing keys or connection strings, adding child resources, and accessing properties such as the domain name or IP address of a resource.

Using a resource later in your template is as simple as using the symbolic name you assigned to your resource. In terms of our storage account, it would be used to, for example, get the list of its keys or the connection string, as shown in the following code:

```
resource stg 'Microsoft.Storage/storageAccounts@2021-02-01' = {
  name: 'mystorage${uniqueString(resourceGroup().id)}'
  location: 'eastus'
  kind: 'StorageV2'
  sku: {
```

```
    name: 'Premium_LRS'
  }
}
resource serverFarm 'Microsoft.Web/serverfarms@2021-02-01' = {
  name: 'ASP'
  location: resourceGroup().location
  sku: {
    name: 'S1'
  }
}
resource azureFunction 'Microsoft.Web/sites@2020-12-01' = {
  name: 'name'
  location: 'eastus'
  kind: 'functionapp'
  properties: {
    serverFarmId: serverFarm.id
    siteConfig: {
      appSettings: [
        {
          name: 'AzureWebJobsStorage'
          value:
'DefaultEndpointsProtocol=https;AccountName=storageAccount-
Name2;AccountKey=${listKeys(stg.id, stg.apiVersion). .keys[0].
value}'
        }
      ]
    }
  }
}
```

> **Note**
> Do not try to deploy the preceding template as it contains placeholder properties.

Pay attention to the application settings section of the Azure Function resource and how it is referencing the storage account object to get its keys. The listKeys function is the same function that is used in an ARM template; we will learn about this in more detail later in this book. This approach is sometimes called **implicit dependency declaration**.

Referencing an already deployed resource

To reference an already deployed resource, all you need to do is use the existing keyword, along with its name. This will tell Bicep to not bother trying to find it in the current template. Instead, it will assume that it has already been deployed:

```
resource stg 'Microsoft.Storage/storageAccounts@2019-06-01'
existing = {
  name: 'myStorage'
}
resource container 'Microsoft.Storage/storageAccounts/
blobServices/containers@2021-02-01' = {
  name: '${stg.name}/default/mycontainer'
  properties: {
    denyEncryptionScopeOverride: true
    defaultEncryptionScope: '$account-encryption-key'
    publicAccess: 'None'
    metadata: {}
  }
}
```

> **Note**
> You cannot have any line breaks within the same statement. Anywhere in this book where you see a line break on the same statement is due to the lack of space in the same line. Bicep uses line breaks to interpret the next item when it is compiling the file. Likewise, you cannot have any trailing commas after statements.

There are a few new items in this snippet that we have not talked about yet. However, put those aside for now and look at the usage of the existing keyword for the storage account. We used it to create a blob container in that storage account.

Explicit dependencies

If you wanted to explicitly specify the dependencies to your resources, you have the dependsOn keyword, similar to what you have in ARM templates:

```
resource appServicePlan 'Microsoft.Web/serverfarms@2020-06-01'
= {
  name: 'ASP'
  location: resourceGroup().location
  sku: {
    name: 'S1'
  }
}
resource appService 'Microsoft.Web/sites@2020-06-01' = {
  name: 'app${uniqueString(resourceGroup().id)}'
  location: resourceGroup().location
  kind: 'app'
  properties: {
    serverFarmId: appServicePlan.id
  }
  dependsOn: [
    appServicePlan
  ]
}
```

This template is explicit about otherZone, depending on the dnsZone resource.

Visualizing dependencies

Using the Bicep extension in VS Code, you can visualize the dependency graph for your resources. Simply click on the tree icon at the top of your open file and view the results. The following screenshot shows the dependency graph from our previous example:

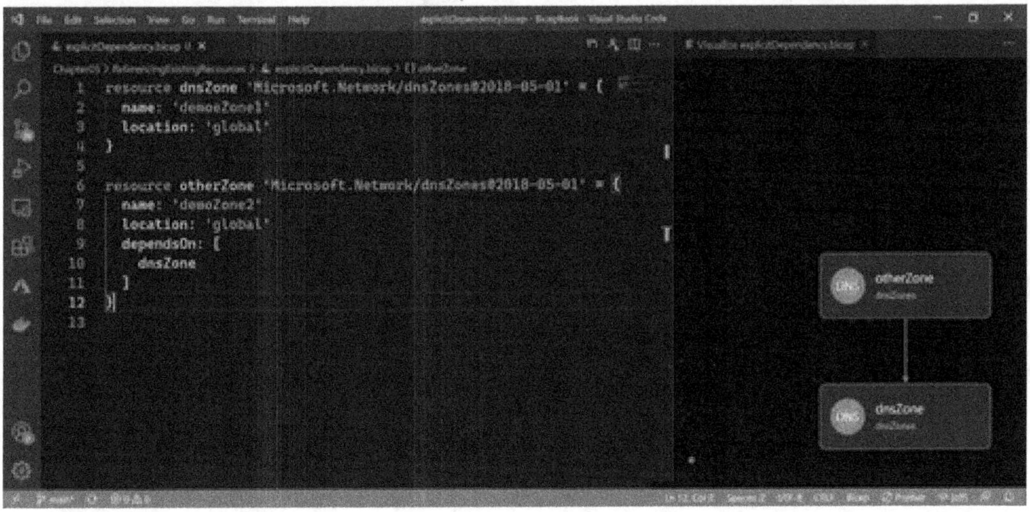

Figure 5.1 – Dependency graph for resources in VS Code

The more we go on, the more you will realize how easy it is to use VS Code to create or work on your templates. In the next section, we will look at the resource scopes in a Bicep file.

Resource scopes

There are four different modes of deployment you can utilize:

- Resource group
- Subscription
- Management group
- Tenant

If you are not familiar with these concepts, feel free to refer to the official documentation at https://docs.microsoft.com/en-us/azure/cloud-adoption-framework/ready/azure-setup-guide/organize-resources?tabs=Azur eManagementGroupsAndHierarchy.

You can deploy your templates at each of these scope levels without specifying the target scope within the file. Each of these scopes would require a command when it comes to deployment, whether you are using the Azure CLI or Azure PowerShell.

For example, in the Azure CLI, for a resource group, it is `az deployment group create`, whereas, for a subscription, it will be `az deployment sub create`.

In Azure PowerShell, different commands will be required, such as `New-AzResourceGroupDeployment` and `New-AzSubscriptionDeployment`. For more details, please visit `https://docs.microsoft.com/en-us/azure/azure-resource-manager/templates/deploy-powershell`.

Now, let's look at these modes in more detail.

Resource group

By default, the resources in your Bicep file are deployed to a resource group. However, you can set the target scope explicitly in your template using the `targetScope` keyword:

```
targetScope = 'resourceGroup'
```

It is not necessary to set the resource group scope explicitly, but this keyword is used for other scopes, which we will review shortly.

Subscription

Not all resources can be deployed to resource groups. For example, blueprints or budgets should be deployed at the subscription level. You can even create the resource group itself in the subscription scope. Here is an example Bicep file targeting a subscription:

```
param principalId string
param roleDefId string = '8e3af657-a8ff-443c-a75c-2fe8c4bcb635'
//owner
targetScope = 'subscription'
resource rg 'Microsoft.Resources/resourceGroups@2020-10-01' = {
  name: 'myResourceGroup'
  location: 'eastus'
}
resource roleAssignment 'Microsoft.Authorization/
roleAssignments@2020-04-01-preview' = {
  name: guid('Owner', principalId, subscription().
subscriptionId)
```

```
properties: {
    roleDefinitionId: subscriptionResourceId('Microsoft.
Authorization/roleDefinitions', roleDefId)
    principalId: principalId
  }
}
```

This Bicep file will create a new resource group within the target subscription, then create a role assignment on that subscription based on the role definition ID and service principal ID passed into it.

The following are a few of the supported resources at the subscription level:

- `artifacts`
- `blueprints`
- `blueprintAssignment`
- `versions (Blueprints)`
- `policyAssignments`
- `policyDefinitions`
- `policySetDefinitions`
- `remediations`
- `roleAssignments`
- `roleDefinitions`
- `deployments`
- `resourceGroups`
- `advisor configurations`
- `budgets`
- `tags`

You might want to apply some of these resources at the management group level. If that is the case, then the next section will help you do this.

Management group

You can deploy a subset of resources at the management group level. Most use cases for management group deployments are role and policy assignments. However, you can also deploy a management group within a management group, given that you have set the parent scope to `tenant`. To set your scope to `managementGroup`, simply use the following line in your template:

```
targetScope = 'managementGroup'
```

Finally, if you want a resource to be effective for the entire organization, then you need to use the tenant scope. We will look at this in the next section.

Tenant

At the tenant level, you may also wish to apply RBAC roles and policies. However, you have a few more options, such as tenant configuration and billing profiles and invoice sections. Simply set your `targetScope` to `tenant` to deploy the content of your Bicep file for the entire organization:

```
targetScope = 'tenant'
resource mgmg 'Microsoft.Management/
managementGroups@2020-02-01' = {
  name: 'myManagementGroup'
}
```

This template would deploy a new management group within your tenant.

Setting the scope at the resource level

You can set the scope of your resource deployment at the resource level as well. As an example, imagine that you wanted to deploy a management group within a management group, as I briefly touched upon previously. Here, you can simply set the scope of your child resource to your parent management group, like so:

```
targetScope = 'managementGroup'

resource parentMG 'Microsoft.Management/
managementGroups@2020-05-01' = {
  name: 'parentGroup'
  scope: tenant()
}
```

```
resource newMG 'Microsoft.Management/
managementGroups@2020-05-01' = {
  scope: tenant()
  name: 'childGroup'
  properties: {
    details: {
      parent: {
        id: parentMG.id
      }
    }
  }
}
```

Here, both management groups have their scope set to the tenant level. However, there is a hierarchy as we are setting the parent for the child management group using its ID. All of this is happening while the main `targetScope` is set to `managementGroup`.

Multi-scope Bicep files

You can also have a Bicep file that can target multiple scopes. This could be an RBAC role assignment that can be applied both at the management group and subscription levels. To achieve this, you can pass an array to `targetScope` instead of a single string value:

```
targetScope = [
  'subscription'
  'managementGroup'
]
```

You have seen a few examples so far where we have used a function as the value for the `scope` property. Those are called global functions and can be used as scopes. Let's see what global functions are available.

Global functions

Here is the list of global functions you can use to pass to the scope property:

Function	Scope
`tenant()`	Returns the tenant scope
`managementGroup()`	Returns the current management group scope
`managementGroup(name: string)`	Returns the scope of a named management group
`subscription()`	Returns the subscription scope of the current deployment
`subscription(subscriptionId: string)`	Returns the scope of a subscription with the specified ID
`resourceGroup()`	Returns the current resource group scope
`resourceGroup(resourceGroupName: string)`	Returns the scope of a named resource group
`resourceGroup(subscriptionId: string, resourceGroupName: name)`	Returns the scope of a named resource group within the specified subscription

You can also specify the scope at the module level, which we will cover in one of our future chapters.

Now that we have covered some basics, let's have a look at Bicep's language specification, what object types are supported, and why that makes Bicep a much better tool to work with.

Bicep language specification

Azure Bicep has its own language, so it is common to have a specification that defines the structure of a Bicep file. Let's start with its structure.

Structure

Any Bicep file can have one or multiple of each of the following declarations:

- Parameters
- Variables
- Resources
- Modules
- Outputs

Each of these items should be separated by a new line. You cannot have a comma or semicolon in a Bicep file as a separator. We will cover these items later in this book.

Whitespaces

Whitespaces and tabs are ignored in Bicep files. However, as we mentioned previously, a new line will have a meaning, even within `object` properties or `array` items.

Comments

You can provide comments by using a double slash (`//`) for single-line comments and `/*` and `*/` for multiline comments:

```
param bool isProd  = true // this is a single line comment


/* this
is a
multi line comment */
```

You also have all the different data types, which we will cover in the next section.

Bicep type system

One of the major benefits of Bicep over ARM templates is that it has native type support. This will not only help with validation and errors being caught early in the development cycle but also makes it easier to convert from Bicep into JSON since all the types are compatible.

Supported data types

The way Bicep supports data type assignability is defined based on the actual type rather than the object's name or characteristics. In other words, the structure of the object's type will determine its type, very much like how `TypeScript` works. However, you need to keep in mind that although Bicep infers the type, it does not perform any automatic conversion, and everything should be defined explicitly.

Simple types

Here are the simple data types supported by Bicep:

- `any`: The value can be anything.
- `error`: The expression contains an error.
- `string`: The value is a string/text.
- `number`: The type is still under development but would represent a floating-point number.
- `int`: The value is a 32-bit integer. This is a subtype of `number` and has no equivalent in JSON.
- `bool`: The value is either `true` or `false`.
- `null`: There is no value or the value is null.

We have already seen some of these types in our previous examples. Here is a refresher:

```
kind: 'StorageV2'
properties: {
    allowBlobPublicAccess: true
}
```

In this code snippet, `kind` is a `string` property and `allowBlobPublicAccess` is a `bool`.

Strings

Strings require their own section since there are some characters you should be careful with. For example, the backslash (\\), single quote ('), line feed (\\n), carriage return (\\r), tab (\\t), Unicode code points (\\u{x}), and dollar sign ($) are all reserved characters and must be escaped when used. Here is an example of using a single quote:

```
var string = 'what\'s your name?'
```

You can also benefit from string interpolation by wrapping your string in '${yourstring}':

```
var storageName = 'storage${uniqueString(resourceGroup().id)}'
```

Next, let us look at multi-line strings.

Multi-line strings

You can have your strings in multiple lines by wrapping them with three single quote characters:

```
var message = '''what\'s
your name?'''
```

Alternatively, you can do the following:

```
var myVar4 = '''
  this
    is
        indented
'''
```

In the preceding code, you have a set of indented strings that is part of the same variable.

Objects

Objects are supported in Bicep and represent any objects that have one or multiple simple type properties or object properties. Here is an example:

```
sku: {
  name: 'Premium_LRS'
}
```

Objects can have other types as the values of their properties.

Arrays

Arrays are another supported type by Bicep that maps to their JSON equivalent. They start with a left bracket ([ ), end with a right bracket ( ]), and represent a collection of items that can involve simple, object, or array objects. For example, an array of integers is denoted by int []. Here is an example that we have used before:

```
virtualNetworkRules: [
    {
        id: 'SUBNET ID'
        action: 'Allow'
    }
]
```

In this code snippet, we have an array of objects. You can also have mixed arrays with values of different types:

```
var mixedArray = [
  100
  true
  'string value'
]
```

In some languages, you cannot have an array that has different types, but here, this is allowed.

Union types

This is a concept that comes from **TypeScript**, but it was introduced way before that, including in **C++** and **PHP 8.0**. It represents a value that can be one of several types. For example, if a value could be either a string or an integer, then it is a union type and is denoted with string | int. Generally, this is used with ternary operations due to multiple values being allowed:

```
param isProdLike bool
var testLocations = [
  'northeurope'
]
var prodLocations = [
  'northeurope'
```

```
    'westeurope'
]
var locations = isProdLike ? prodLocations : testLocations
```

In the preceding code snippet, the expression would be evaluated to `string[] |`
`array`. Now is a good time to provide a quick comparison between ARM and Bicep
syntax.

ARM and Bicep syntax comparison

Bicep has some syntax in common with ARM templates, though some simplifications
have been made, as shown in the following table:

Scenario	ARM Template	Bicep
Expressions	`[func()]`	`func()`
Concatenation	`concat('Test', ' ', parameters('paramName'))`	`'Test ${paramName}'`
Logical AND of multiple values	`and(parameter('isProd'), parameter('isReadOnly'))`	`isProd && isReadOnly`
Get the resource ID of a resource in the same template	`resourceId('Microsoft.Storage/ storageAccounts')`	`res.id`
Get the property of a resource	`reference('resourceName').properties. property`	`res.properties. property`
Conditionally decide on a value	`and(parameter('isProd'), 'true value', 'false value')`	`isProd ? 'true value': 'false value'`
Conditionally deploy a resource	`"condition": "[parameter('isProd')]"`	`resource res '…' = if(isProd){…}`
Create reusable templates	Use linked templates	Use modules
Set the target scope to a subscription	`"$schema": " https://schema. management.azure.com/schemas/2018- 05-01/subscriptionDeploymentTemplate. json#"`	`targetScope = 'subscription'`
Set a dependency between resources	`"dependsOn": ["[resourceId('Microsoft. Storage/storageAccounts', 'parameters('storageAccountName'))]"]`	Either use `dependsOn` or implicitly infer it
Iterate arrays	Use `copy`	Use a `for … in …` loop
Get a reference to an existing resource	For each property, use `reference(resourceId(...)).*`	Use the `existing` keyword

Now, let's look at some points you need to keep in mind if you wish to have a better coding standard in your team and cleaner templates.

Best practices for Bicep syntax

There are points you need to be cautious of regarding the Bicep syntax. First things first, avoid using `reference` or `referenceId` unless it's necessary. Your dependencies will either be implicitly inferred when you use a property of a resource or you use the `dependsOn` attribute.

Next, choose a casing standard for your team and stick with it. Many folks like camel case, and that is what the Bicep team uses as well:

```
var myCamelCaseVariable = 'Hi there!'
```

And last but not least, if you intend to add a description to a parameter, make sure it outlines what this parameter is used for to prevent confusion and the risk of passing the wrong value in.

Summary

This chapter has been a great start and has hopefully given you enough insights into how to start writing your Bicep files. We started with how to define resources, then reviewed how to reference existing resources. Then, we looked at resource scopes, followed by the language specification and all the supported types in Bicep. Finally, we provided a quick comparison between the ARM and Bicep syntax and looked at some best practices concerning this. There are still many things we have not covered yet, but we have pointed out parameters, variables, and more. We will cover these in the next chapter. However, before you continue, take a break – you've earned it.

6

Using Parameters, Variables, and Template Functions

Now that you know how to define your resources, it is time to go through some of the concepts that we used but skipped, such as parameters and variables. In this chapter, we will start with parameters first, since you will need them to reuse your templates for different environments and to customize your resources.

Then we'll outline the template variables and how they will help you to keep your templates clean and enable you to have a better coding standard. And finally, we will review the template functions and when they come into the picture.

In this chapter, we are going to cover the following main topics:

- Parameters
- Variables
- Functions

Technical requirements

To take full advantage of this chapter, you will need to have access to a personal computer or laptop that has Visual Studio Code and PowerShell Core installed. The code used throughout this chapter is stored in the GitHub repository at `https://github.com/PacktPublishing/Infrastructure-as-Code-with-Azure-Bicep/tree/main/Chapter06`

Parameters

If you want to leverage the power of infrastructure as code, which is **reusability**, you need to be able to pass parameters to customize the resources for different environments. The first thing **Azure Resource Manager** does before deployment is to have a look at the templates and resolve their values. Then, within the template, it looks for each usage of the parameter and replaces that with the actual value, then starts the deployment.

Setting a type for each parameter is mandatory and you can define them in multiple ways.

Minimalistic definition

The least you must declare for your parameters is a name and a type:

```
param isProd bool
param storageName string
```

The name of the parameter cannot be the same as any other name in the same template, such as a variable, resource, function, or other parameters.

Setting default values

At times, you might like to add a default value in case the user did not pass any value to your deployment. This can also mean the parameter is not mandatory. To use a default value, simply assign a value of the same type to the parameter:

```
param isProd bool = false
```

You can also use expressions as the value for your parameters, which we will review in the next chapter, but as a quick example, here is how you can assign a unique name to the storage account parameter we used earlier:

```
param storageName string = 'sa${ uniqueString(resourceGroup().id))}'
```

You can also decorate your parameters, which is explained in the next section.

Using decorators

When you need to add metadata or any limitation on your parameter, you can use decorators. Decorators are placed above the parameter declaration and should be used in the form of @expression, where expression would be a function call:

```
@expression
param isProd bool
```

There are many decorators you can use, depending on which problem you are trying to solve, but let's start with the most common use case, which is secure parameters.

Secure parameters

Like ARM templates, where secureString and secureObject are supported, Bicep also has a decorator called @secure that allows you to enhance your template by making sure the value passed as these parameters is not saved in the deployment history or logs. Here is an example of a secureString and secureObject parameter passed into the template:

```
@secure
param vmPassword string
@secure
param workflowParameter object
```

> **Note**
>
> If you set a secure value (string or object) to a property that does not expect a secure value, then your value will be treated as plain text.

At times, you might want to limit the values users can pass into the template, such as what type of storage account they can choose, or what virtual machine sku they can select. You can use allowed values for that purpose, which is described in the next section.

Allowed values

Allowed values are expressed using the @allowed function. You can pass an array of values into the function as the list of allowed parameter values:

```
@allowed([
        'Free'
        'Basic'
        'Standard'
])
param appServicePlanSku string
```

This will be evaluated at deployment time and if the value passed into the template is not part of the allowed values, an error will be raised.

You do not have to only pass a string into the allowed value decorator; let's see an example of when you use an object:

```
@allowed([
   {
     location: 'Australia Southeast'
     sku: 'Standard_LRS'
   }
   {
     location: 'Australia East'
     sku: 'Standard_GZRS'
   }
])
param storageAccountSettings array
```

In the preceding code snippet, you are leveraging an object to limit both location and sku properties and a storage account.

You can also limit the length of your string or array parameters; if that is your use case, read on.

String and array length constraints

Any string or array parameter can have limitations on its length. These will be checked prior to deployment at compile time and the corresponding error will be raised if the passed parameter does not comply with the restrictions. To limit the length, use the @ minLength and @maxLength functions:

```
@minLength(5)
@maxLength(20)
param appServiceName string

@minLength(1)
@maxLength(5)
param appNames array
```

The preceding snippet will accept a parameter for the app service name, which is 5 to 20 characters long. The appNames array also will be restricted from 1 to 5 items in total.

Similarly, you can limit an integer parameter.

Integer value constraints

Any integer parameter can be checked to be between a minimum and maximum value. This can be done using @minValue and @maxValue attributes as follows:

```
@minValue(1)
@maxValue(10)
param appServicePlanInstanceCount int
```

The preceding snippet forced users to choose a value between 1 and 10 inclusive for how many instances of the app service plan are going to be created. This restriction will also be evaluated at compile time before the deployment happens. Now let's see how you can add metadata to your parameters.

Metadata

Any parameter can have metadata attached to it. You can do so using the `@metadata` attribute and you can pass an object to the function as well:

```
@metadata({
  description: 'This parameter is used to specify the network
rules for the storage account'
})
param networkRule object
```

You can add any property to the object you pass to the `@metadata` function; however, for `description`, there is also a dedicated decorator.

Description

If we wanted to add a description to any parameter, we would use the `@description` decorator. Let's revise the previous example:

```
@ description('This parameter is used to specify the network
rules for the storage account')
param networkRule object
```

If your requirements need you to, you can combine multiple decorators on the same parameter as well.

Combining decorators

You can combine multiple parameters to enforce multiple restrictions or add metadata to the parameter if you want:

```
@minLength(3)
@maxLength(24)
@description('Name of the storage account')
param storageAccountName string =
 'sa${uniqueString(resourceGroup().id)}'
```

Decorators are very powerful, and I recommend you use them when applicable to have much better control over your parameters before and during the deployment. Now let's see how you can use these parameters within the template.

Using parameters within a Bicep template

To use the value of a parameter, simply use its name in your template:

```
@minLength(3)
@maxLength(24)
@description('Name of the storage account')
param storageAccountName string =
'sa${uniqueString(resourceGroup().id)}'


param location string = resourceGroup().location


resource stg 'Microsoft.Storage/storageAccounts@2021-02-01' = {
  name: storageAccountName
  location: location
  kind: 'StorageV2'
  sku: {
    name: 'Premium_LRS'
  }
}
```

You can also pass objects as parameters, so let's see an example of that:

```
@allowed([
  {
    location: 'East US'
    sku: 'Standard_LRS'
  }
  {
    location: 'West US'
    sku: 'Standard_GRS'
  }
])
param storageAccountSettings array


resource storageaccount 'Microsoft.Storage/
storageAccounts@2021-02-01' = {
  name: 'name'
  location: storageAccountSettings[0].location
```

```
kind: 'StorageV2'
sku: {
  name: storageAccountSettings[0].sku
}
}
```

You can see how easy it is to define, limit, enrich, and use parameters in a Bicep file. Now it is time to see how we can pass parameters during deployment.

Passing parameters during deployment

There are two ways you can pass parameters into the Bicep file during deployment, regardless of whether you are using Azure CLI or Azure PowerShell: inline, and as a separate file.

Inline

You can pass parameters inline during deployment. Here is an example using Azure CLI:

```
az deployment group what-if `
  --resource-group Bicep `
  --template-file main.bicep `
  --parameter storageAccountName="uniquestring"
storageAccountSettings="[{'location':'Australia Southeast',
'sku': 'Standard_LRS'}]"
```

You can find these examples in the GitHub repository in the chapter06 folder.

> **Note**
>
> The preceding script is written to be used in a PowerShell terminal; if you are using bash, replace the single quotes with double quotes and double quotes with single quotes.

If you are using Azure PowerShell, you can pass the parameters in as follows:

```
New-AzResourceGroupDeployment -ResourceGroupName Bicep `
  -Whatif `
  -TemplateFile main.bicep `
  -storageAccountName "uniquestring"
```

To pass an array of objects in PowerShell, you would need to create a hash table object and pass it in:

```
$arrayParam = @{ location = "Australia Southeast"; sku =
"Standard_LRS"}
New-AzResourceGroupDeployment -ResourceGroupName Bicep `
  -Whatif `
  -TemplateFile main.bicep `
  -storageAccountName "uniquestring" `
  -storageAccountSettings $arrayParam
```

You can also pass these parameters from a file.

Parameter file

You could also use a parameter file to pass in your templates. Bicep does not have a custom template file structure; it uses the same template file you use for your ARM templates. That gives you the ability to reuse your template files:

```
{
   "$schema": "https://schema.management.azure.com/
schemas/2019-04-01/deploymentParameters.json#",
   "contentVersion": "1.0.0.0",
   "parameters": {
     "storageAccountName": {
       "value": "uniquestring"
     },
     "storageAccountSettings": {
       "value": [
         {
           "location": "Australia East",
           "sku": "Standard_ZRS"
         }
       ]
     }
   }
}
```

Now you can pass the file in your deployment instead of providing the parameters one by one. Here is how to pass it into the Azure CLI command:

```
az deployment group what-if `
  --resource-group Bicep `
  --template-file main.bicep `
  --parameters ./main.parameters.json
```

And this is how to pass it in Azure PowerShell:

```
New-AzResourceGroupDeployment -ResourceGroupName Bicep `
  -Whatif `
  -TemplateFile main.bicep `
  -TemplateParameterFile ./main.parameters.json
```

If you have any mismatch between parameters, are missing any required ones, or have a type mismatch issue, you will be notified right away, which really helps to catch these types of issues upfront.

But enough about parameters, let's review variables and when to use them.

Variables

Variables comes into play when you do not have a straightforward value but rather a complicated expression. Instead of repeating this complex expression within your Bicep files even if it is just one time, you can define a variable that contains this expression. Then use the variable anywhere you need that value within your template.

Azure Resource Manager will resolve the value right before starting the deployment, then replace any occurrence of the variable with that value. So let's see how you define variables.

Defining variables

Unlike parameters, you do not need to provide a type when defining variables:

```
var storageAccountName = 'name'
```

You start with the reserved keyword var, then a name for your variable, and finally the value you want to assign to it. You can have variables of any type within your template:

```
var isProd = true
var appServicePlanInstanceCount = 5
var storageSkus = createArray('Standard_LRS', 'Standard_ZRS', 'Premium_GRS')
```

You can reuse a variable or parameter to form the value of another variable.

Reusing variables in other variables

You can use string interpolation for strings or other functions to reuse a variable to create other variables:

```
param environmentName string = 'prod'
var stroageAccountName =
'${environmentName}${uniqueString(resourceGroup().id)}sa'
```

Now that you have your value set up, you can use it within your template.

Using variables

To use a variable, like a parameter, just use its name:

```
param rgLocation string = resourceGroup().location
param environmentName string = 'prod'
var storageName =
'${environmentName}${uniqueString(resourceGroup().id)}sa'
resource stg 'Microsoft.Storage/storageAccounts@2021-02-01' = {
  name: storageName
  location: rgLocation
  kind: 'Storage'
  sku: {
    name: 'Standard_LRS'
  }
}
```

You can define as many variables as necessary and use them within your templates. They can be any type and if you pass them to those properties expecting those types, you will not have any issues.

There is another use case for variables, which is to have multiple sets to choose from depending on a condition.

Configuration variables

Think about a situation where you are reusing the template for multiple environments. Instead of defining multiple values for each one, you can define one for all and then choose which one to use based on a parameter or another variable. The following example shows the usage of this pattern:

```
@allowed([
  'test'
  'prod'
])
param environmentName string

var environmentSettings = {
  test: {
    appServicePlanSku: 'S1'
    instanceCount: 1
  }
  prod: {
    appServicePlanSku: 'P1'
    instanceCount: 4
  }
}

resource appServicePlan 'Microsoft.Web/serverfarms@2020-12-01' = {
  name: 'name'
  location: resourceGroup().location
  sku: {
    name: environmentSettings[environmentName].appServicePlanSku
```

```
    capacity: environmentSettings[environmentName].
  instanceCount
    }
  }
```

This template allows you to select a different value set based on the parameter you will pass into it. It is a very useful pattern, especially if you mix it with modules, which we will review later.

Now it's time to review template functions.

Template functions

There are many functions that you can leverage to enhance your template. These functions give you the ability to create complex expressions or dynamic values to be used later in the template. Many of these functions work with specific data types that we have seen before, such as arrays, strings, objects, and integers. However, there are also functions that are designed to help you create logical flows or get a scope to apply your template to. Let's start with generic functions first.

The any function

The any function allows you to resolve issues around data types when you are not sure of a property's type. This could be in a case when the property expects you to pass an integer, but you need to pass it as a string, that is, ('0.5'). Here is an example of the any function in practice:

```
publicIPAddress: any((pipId == '') ? null : {
   id: pipId
})
```

This function can be assigned to any value in Bicep. Date functions are the next to be reviewed.

Date functions

There are two functions you can use if you are working with dates: dateTimeAdd and utcNow. An example of using both functions would be as follows:

```
param baseTime string = utcNow('u')
var add3Years = dateTimeAdd(baseTime, 'P3Y')
```

As you might have guessed, `utcNow` returns the current date time in the specified format. It accepts the format as input that can be found at `https://docs.microsoft.com/en-us/dotnet/standard/base-types/standard-date-and-time-format-strings`. If no format is passed, it will return the ISO 8601, which is `yyyMMddTHHmmssZ`.

The `dateTimeAdd` function gets a date and adds the time specified to that date, then returns the result. The function definition is as follows:

```
dateTimeAdd(base, duration, [format])
```

`base` is the starting date time, `duration` is how long should be added to the base, and `format`, which is optional, will specify the output format. If you do not specify the format, the format of base value will be used. Now let's see the `bool` function.

The bool function

The `bool` function converts the parameter to a `boolean`. You can pass a string or integer to this function and the result is shown in the following example:

```
var trueString = bool('true')
var falseString = bool('false')
var trueInt = bool(1)
var falseInt = bool(0)
```

You can mix this function with logical operators to form conditional expressions, which can be helpful in deciding whether a resource should be deployed or not or other similar use cases.

We will review these in the next chapter.

Deployment functions

Deployment functions help you to get information about the current deployment or environment. The `deployment` function returns an object as follows:

```
{
    "name": "",
    "properties": {
        "template": {
            "$schema": "",
            "contentVersion": "",
```

```
        "parameters": {},
        "variables": {},
        "resources": [],
        "outputs": {}
      },
      "templateHash": "",
      "parameters": {},
      "mode": "",
      "provisioningState": ""
    }
}
```

This value is returned when the deployment scope is a resource group. If you are deploying to a subscription or management group, then the following will be returned:

```
{
  "name": "",
  "location": "",
  "properties": {
    "template": {
      "$schema": "",
      "contentVersion": "",
      "resources": [],
      "outputs": {}
    },
    "templateHash": "",
    "parameters": {},
    "mode": "",
    "provisioningState": ""
  }
}
```

The environment function will return information about the Azure environment used for deployment. An example of the return value will be as follows:

```
{
  "name": "",
  "gallery": "",
```

```
    "graph": "",
    "portal": "",
    "graphAudience": "",
    "activeDirectoryDataLake": "",
    "batch": "",
    "media": "",
    "sqlManagement": "",
    "vmImageAliasDoc": "",
    "resourceManager": "",
    "authentication": {
      "loginEndpoint": "",
      "audiences": [
        "",
        ""
      ],
      "tenant": "",
      "identityProvider": ""
    },
    "suffixes": {
      "acrLoginServer": "",
      "azureDatalakeAnalyticsCatalogAndJob": "",
      "azureDatalakeStoreFileSystem": "",
      "azureFrontDoorEndpointSuffix": "",
      "keyvaultDns": "",
      "sqlServerHostname": "",
      "storage": ""
    }
}
```

Next, we'll have a look at numeric functions.

Numeric functions

There are three numeric functions available in Bicep: int, min, and max. The int function converts the passed parameter to an integer:

```
output inResult int = int('4')
```

The min function gets either an array of integers or a comma-separated list and returns the smallest value:

```
param intArray array = [
  2
  5
  4
]
output arrayMinValue int = min(arrayToTest)
output listMinValue int = min(3,2,5,4)
```

Both arrayMinValue and listMinValue will have the value of 2 after the deployment is run.

And the max function will be like the min function, but it returns the maximum value. Let's review array functions next.

Array functions

There are many functions that help you work with arrays. The following table lists each function and its description:

Function	Description
`array(arg1)`	Converts a value to an array; it can receive `int`, `string`, `array`, or `object`.
`concat(arg1, arg2, arg3, ...)`	Combines multiple `array` values and returns the result.
`contains(container, itemToFind)`	Checks whether an `array` contains a value, or an `object` contains a key, or a `string` contains a character. When checking strings, the comparison is case-sensitive whereas with object keys it is `case-insensitive`.
`empty(item)`	Determines whether an `array`, `object`, or `string` is empty.
`first(arg1)`	Returns the first item in an `array` or the first character in a `string`.
`intersection(arg1, arg2, arg3, ...)`	Returns a single `array` or `object` with common elements of passed parameters.
`last(arg1)`	Returns the last element of an `array` or the last character of a `string`.
`length(arg1)`	Returns the number of elements in an `array`, or characters in a `string`, or the root-level properties of an `object`.
`max(arg1)`	Returns the maximum value of an `array` or a comma-separated list of integers.
`min(arg1)`	Returns the minimum value of an `array` or a comma-separated list of integers.
`range(startIndex, count)`	Creates an array of integers from a starting number that contains the number of items passed by the `count` parameter.
`skip(originalValue, numberToSkip)`	Returns an `array` with all elements after the specified number, or a `string` with all characters after a specified number in the `string`.
`take(originalValue, numberToTake)`	Returns an `array` with the specified number of elements from the start, or a `string` with the specified number of characters from the start.
`union(arg1, arg2, arg3, ...)`	Returns a single `array` or `object` with all elements from the parameters. Duplicate keys or values are omitted.

Table 6.1 – Array functions

> **Note**
> The preceding definitions have all been copied directly from the Microsoft documentation that can be found at `https://docs.microsoft.com/en-us/azure/azure-resource-manager/bicep/bicep-functions-array`.

You can find an example of each function in the following code block:

```
var fruits = [
  'orange'
  'apple'
]

var smoothies = [
  'pineapple'
  'mango'
]

var person = {
  'name': 'James'
  'lastName': 'Bond'
}

//array
output intOutput array = array(1) // [1]
output stringOutput array = array('test') // ["test"]
output objectOutput array = array({
  'name': 'John'
  'lastName': 'Doe'
}) // [{"name": "John", "lastName": "Doe"}]

//concat
output concatanatedArray array = concat(fruits, smoothies) //
["orange", "apple", "pineapple", "mango"]

//contains
output stringTrue bool = contains('test', 'e') // true
output objectTrue bool = contains(person, 'name') // true
output arrayFalse bool = contains(fruits, 'banana') // false

//empty
output arrayEmpty bool = empty([]) // true
output objectEmpty bool = empty({}) // true
```

```
output stringEmpty bool = empty('') // true
...
```

You can find the complete version of the code block at the book's GitHub repository at `Chapter06/Functions/array.bicep` in the book's GitHub repository.

Now let's review `object` functions.

Object functions

There are several functions that allow you to work with objects. The following table summarizes them, and is followed by their example code snippets:

Function	Description
contains(container, itemToFind)	This function checks whether an object contains a value, a key, or a string contains a substring. The string comparison is case-sensitive and for objects is case-insensitive.
empty(object)	Checks whether the object is empty or not. We reviewed this function earlier on within the array functions.
intersection(arg1, arg2, arg3, …)	This function returns an object with the common elements from the parameters.
json(arg1)	Converts a valid JSON string to a JSON data type.
length(arg1)	Returns the number of top-level properties in an object. We reviewed this function also within the array functions.
union(arg1, arg2, arg3, …)	This function returns a single object from all the input parameters. The duplicated keys are omitted. This function was also reviewed within the array functions.

Table 6.2 – Object functions

The following code snippet shows an example of the use of these functions, which you can find in the GitHub repository as well:

```
var spy = {
  'name': 'James'
  'lastName': 'Bond'
  'nationality': 'British'
}
var agent = {
  'name': 'Joe'
  'lastName': 'Walley'
  'nationality': 'British'
```

```
}
```

```
//contain
output containsOutput bool = contains(spy, 'name') // true
```

```
//empty
output objectEmpty bool = empty({}) // true
output objectNotEmpty bool = empty(spy) // false
```

```
//intersection
output intersect object = intersection(spy, agent) //
{'nationality':'British'}
```

You can find the complete code at `Chapter06/Functions/objects.bicep` in the book's GitHub repository.

Now it's time to look at the resource functions, which are very helpful to get resource values in your templates.

Resource functions

Resource functions allow you to retrieve values in your template during deployment. Let's review them one by one this time as these require a bit more explanation.

The extensionResourceId function

This function returns the resource ID for an extension that is added to another resource. An example would be policy deployed to a management group.

The signature of this function is as follows:

```
extensionResourceId(resourceId, resourceType, resourceName1,
[resourceName2], ...)
```

The return value is a resource ID that can be used in your template when needed. A basic format would be as follows:

```
{scope}/providers/{extensionResourceProviderNamespace}/
{extensionResourceType}/{extensionResourceName}
```

The getSecret function

This function gets a secret from a key vault. The signature of this function is as follows:

```
keyVaultName.getSecret(secretName)
```

You can find an example of the usage in the `Chapter06/Functions/Resource/getSecret` folder in the book's GitHub repository.

The list* function

This function will be available on any resource that has a list operation such as `list`, `listKeys`, `listKeyValue`, and `listSecrets`. The syntax varies resource by resource, and if you are trying to get autocomplete for these functions in your Bicep templates, you're out of luck for now. The team is working on this to add support in the future. Here is a generic signature:

```
resourceName.list([apiVersion], [function Values])
```

> **Note**
>
> If you use the `list` function on a resource that is conditionally deployed, it gets evaluated even though your resource might not be deployed at all. You can use the conditional expression (`? :`) operator to make sure the function is only evaluated when the resource is being deployed.

Here is an example of its usage on a `storage account` to get the list of its keys to be used later in a `function app`:

```
resource stg 'Microsoft.Storage/storageAccounts@2019-06-01' = {
  name: 'dscript${uniqueString(resourceGroup().id)}'
  location: resourceGroup().location
  kind: 'StorageV2'
  sku: {
    name: 'Standard_LRS'
  }
}
resource serverFarm 'Microsoft.Web/serverfarms@2021-02-01' existing = {
  name: 'ASP'
```

```
}
resource azureFunction 'Microsoft.Web/sites@2020-12-01' = {
  name: 'name'
  location: resourceGroup().location
  kind: 'functionapp'
  properties: {
    serverFarmId: serverFarm.id
    siteConfig: {
      appSettings: [
        {
          name: 'AzureWebJobsDashboard'
          value: 'DefaultEndpointsProtocol=https;AccountName=
storageAccountName1;AccountKey=${stg.listKeys().keys[0].value}'
        }
        {
          name: 'AzureWebJobsStorage'
          value: 'DefaultEndpointsProtocol=https;AccountName=
storageAccountName1;AccountKey=${stg.listKeys().keys[0].value}'
        }
      ]
    }
  }
}
```

Now let's review the `pickZones` function.

The pickZones function

This function determines whether a resource supports *zones* in a *region*. If you are not familiar with the concepts of availability zones, refer to the documentation at https://azure.microsoft.com/en-au/global-infrastructure/availability-zones/.

The signature of this function is as follows:

```
pickZones(providerNamespace, resourceType, location,
[numberOfZones], [offset])
```

The function returns an empty array when the region does not support zones, or an array with the number of zones inside:

```
output supported array = pickZones('Microsoft.Compute',
'virtualMachines', 'westus2') // ["1"]
output notSupportedRegion array = pickZones('Microsoft.
Compute', 'virtualMachines', 'northcentralus') // []
```

You also have some additional functions, which we will review next.

Resource ID functions

There are four functions that help you get a resource: `reference`, `resourceId`, `subscriptionResourceId`, and `tenantResourceId`. You normally do not need these functions since you can easily use the existing keyword with the name of the resource to get a reference. But if you do, feel free to check out the documentation at `https://docs.microsoft.com/en-us/azure/azure-resource-manager/bicep/bicep-functions-resource#reference`.

And lastly, we need to review the string functions.

String functions

There are many functions available to work with strings. You can find the list in the following table:

Function	Description
`base64(inputString)`	Returns the `base64` representation of an input string.
`base64ToJson(base64)`	Returns the `object` representation of a `base64` string.
`base64ToString(base64)`	Returns the string representation of a `base64` string.
`concat`	Instead of using the `concat` function, uses string interpolation.
`contains(container, itemToFind)`	This function determines whether a string contains a substring. The comparison is case-sensitive.
`dataUri(string)`	This function converts a value to a `data URI`.
`dataUriToString(dataUri)`	This function converts a data URI to a string.
`empty(string)`	Checks whether a string is empty or not.

Function	Description
`endsWith(string, stringToFind)`	Checks whether a string ends with a value.
`first(arg1)`	Returns the first character of the string.
`format(string, arg1, arg2, ...)`	Creates a formatted string from the input values.
`guid(baseString, ...)`	Creates a value in the format of a globally unique identifier based on the parameters. The passed parameter limits the uniqueness of the result.
`indexOf(search, find)`	Returns the first position of a value within a string. The comparison is case-insensitive, zero-based, and if the value is not found, -1 is returned.
`json(arg1)`	Converts a value JSON string into a JSON object.
`last(arg1)`	Returns the last character of a string.
`lastIndexOf(search, find)`	Returns the last position of a value within a string. The comparison is case-insensitive, zero-based, and if the value is not found, -1 is returned.
`length(string)`	Returns the length of a string.
`newGuid()`	Returns a globally unique identifier. This function can only be used in the default value of a parameter.
`padLeft(value, total, char)`	Returns a right-aligned string by adding a passed character to the left until the length reaches the value of the total patameter.
`replace(origin, old, new)`	Replaces a new value with all instances of the old value in a string.
`skip(origin, numberToSkip)`	Returns a string with all characters after the specified number of characters.
`split(input, delimiter)`	Returns an array of strings that contains substrings separated by the delimiter in the original string.
`startsWith(search, find)`	Determines whether a string starts with a value and is case-insensitive.
`string(value)`	Converts a value to `string`.
`substring(string, startIndex, length)`	Returns a substring of the original string starting at the given index and of the specified length.
`take(origin, numberToTake)`	Returns a string with the specified number of characters from the start of the string.
`toLower(string)`	Converts a string to lowercase.

Function	Description
`toUpper(string)`	Converts a string to uppercase.
`trim(string)`	Removes all leading and trailing white spaces from a string.
`uniqueString(baseString, ...)`	Creates a deterministic hash string based on provided parameters.
`uri(baseUri, relativeUri)`	Creates an absolute URI based on the provided parameters.
`uriComponent(string)`	Encodes a URI.
`uriComponentToString(uri)`	Returns a string of a URI-encoded value.

Table 6.3 – String functions

> **Note**
>
> The definition of the preceding functions is copied from the official Microsoft documentation, which can be found at `https://docs.microsoft.com/en-us/azure/azure-resource-manager/bicep/bicep-functions-string`.

And lastly, here are all the examples of these string functions, which you can also find in the GitHub repository:

```
//base64
output base64Output string = base64('one, two, three') //
b25lLCB0d28sIHRocmVl
```

```
//base64ToJson
output toJsonOutput object =
base64ToJson('b25lLCB0d28sIHRocmVl') // {"one": "a", "two":
"b"}
```

```
//base64ToString
output toStringOutput string =
base64ToString('b25lLCB0d28sIHRocmVl') //'one, two, three'
```

```
//concat
param prefix string = 'prefix'
```

```
output concatOutput string = '${prefix}
And${uniqueString(resourceGroup().id)}'
...
```

You can find the complete code examples in the `Chapter06/Functions/string.bicep` file in the book's GitHub repository.

All these functions are designed to help you write better templates and make your job easier; however, there is no need to overuse them unnecessarily.

Summary

By finishing this chapter, you have expanded your knowledge of **Azure Bicep** by reviewing how to use parameters to reuse your templates to create multiple environments. Then you learned how to use variables to prevent repeating complex expressions throughout your templates and create clean and maintainable Bicep files. And lastly, you found out about all sorts of different functions that are available for you to leverage and work with different data types, access resources, create logic, and get the property values of existing resources within your template for further use.

In the next chapter, we will expand on expressions and what can be achieved, creating logic and using conditions and loops to make even more powerful templates.

7

Understanding Expressions, Symbolic Names, Conditions, and Loops

Knowing how to create resources, use parameters and variables to form resource names and properties, and use functions is not enough to create complex scenarios. In this chapter, we will learn about expressions and all the supported operators you can use to control their deployment or flow. Then, we will look at conditions and loops, which you can use to address some situations where you might need to create multiple copies of the same resource with different properties.

After completing this chapter, you should be able to fully leverage the power of reusable templates and be able to not only write great Bicep files but also help others in your team to do the same.

In this chapter, we are going to cover the following main topics:

- Understanding expressions
- Exploring conditions
- Diving into resource iterations

Technical requirements

To take full advantage of this chapter, you will need to have access to a personal computer or laptop that has Visual Studio Code and PowerShell core installed. The code for this chapter is stored in this book's GitHub repository at `https://github.com/PacktPublishing/Infrastructure-as-Code-with-Azure-Bicep/tree/main/Chapter07`.

Understanding expressions

Azure Bicep supports a variety of expressions and operators that will help you create more dynamic templates and flows within your deployment, whether it is to decide which resource gets deployed and which ones do not, or when you are accessing elements within an object or array to calculate values.

Let's start with unary operators.

Unary operators

There are two unary operators, unary NOT (`!`) and unary minus (`-`), both of which operate on a single operand.

Unary NOT

This operator negates the specified value and is equivalent to the `not` function in ARM templates. Here is an example:

```
param isProd bool = true
var shouldDeployFirewall = !isProd
```

In the preceding code snippet, the value of the `shouldDeployFirewall` variable would be `false`, which can be used later to decide whether to deploy a firewall or not.

Unary minus

This operator multiplies the operand by `-1`. The result of applying this operator to a positive integer returns a negative value and vice versa:

```
param negInt int = -20
output posOutput int = -negInt
```

During the deployment, the `negInt` parameter will contain `-20` and the `posOutput` parameter will contain `20`.

Now, let's review the binary operators.

Comparison operators

These operators can help you compare variables and parameters and return either `true` or `false`. All the supported comparison operators are listed in the following table:

Symbol	Name	Operand Types	Return Type	Template Equivalent	Description
>=	Greater than or equal to	`<string,string>` or `<integer,integer>`	`bool`	`greaterOrEqual (v1, v2)`	Returns `true` if v1 is greater than or equal to v2. Otherwise, `false`. It works with strings and numbers.
>	Greater than	`<string,string>` or `<integer,integer>`	`bool`	`greater(v1, v2)`	Returns `true` if v1 is greater than v2. Otherwise, `false`. It works with strings and numbers.

Symbol	Name	Operand Types	Return Type	Template Equivalent	Description
`<=`	Less than or equal to	`<string,string>` or `<integer,integer>`	`bool`	`lessOrEquals (v1, v2)`	Returns `true` if v1 is less than or equal to v2. Otherwise, `false`. It works with strings and numbers.
`<`	Less than	`<string,string>` or `<integer,integer>`	`bool`	`less(v1, v2)`	Returns `true` if v1 is less than v2. Otherwise, `false`. Works with both strings and integers.
`==`	Equals	`any any`	`bool`	`equals(v1, v2)`	Returns `true` if the two values are equal. Otherwise, `false`.
`!=`	Not equal	`any any`	`bool`	`not (equals (v1, v2))`	Returns `true` if the two values are not equal. Otherwise. `false`.
`=~`	Equals (case-insensitive)	`<string,string>`	`bool`	`equals( toLower(v1), toLower(v2))`	Returns `true` if the values are equal, ignoring any casing. Otherwise, `false`.
`!~`	Not equals (case-insensitive)	`<string,string>`	`bool`	`not (equals( toLower(v1), toLower(v2)))`	Returns `true` if the values are not equal, ignoring any casing. Otherwise, `false`.

Table 7.1 – Binary comparison operators

Here are a few examples of using these comparison operators:

```
// >=
param appServiceCount int = 2
var shouldCreateScaling = appServiceCount >= 2

output appScalingEnabled bool = shouldCreateScaling // true

// >
param appServicePlanCount int = 3
var moreThanOne = appServicePlanCount > 1

output moreThanOneAppPlan bool = moreThanOne // false
...
```

To see a complete set of examples, please refer to Chapter07/comparison.bicep in this book's GitHub repository.

In addition to these operators, you also have access to several logical operators, so let's review them next.

Logical operators

Logical operators help you evaluate `boolean` expressions or values, figure out whether a value is null or not, or evaluate conditional expressions.

You can find all the supported logical operators in the following table:

Symbol	Name	Operand Types	Return Type	Template Equivalent	Description
`&&`	Logical AND	`<boolean,boolean>`	`bool`	`and(v1, v2)`	Returns `true` if both are `true`; otherwise, it returns `false`. You can have any `boolean` expression on either side of this operator.
`||`	Logical OR	`bool bool`	`bool`	`or(v1, v2)`	Returns `true` if any of the values are `true` and returns `false` when all the values are `false`. You can have any `boolean` expression on either side of this operator.
`!`	NOT	`bool`	`bool`	`not(val)`	Negates the value.
`??`	Coalesce	`any*n`	`any`	`coalesce(val1, ...)`	Returns the first non-`null` value from the parameters.
`?:`	Conditional expression	`bool any any`	`true val | false val`	`if(condition, true val, false val)`	Returns a value based on whether the condition is met or not.

Table 7.2 – Logical operators

Here are a few examples to make it easier to see how these operators work:

```
// &&
param isProd bool = true
param numberOfVMs int = 5
output andResultExp bool = isProd && numberOfVMs > 2 // true


// ||
output prodOrMoreThan5Vms bool = isProd || numberOfVMs >= 5 //
true
// ?:
param properties object = {
```

```
  isProd: false

  numberOfProdApps: 10

  numberOfNonProdAppsNull: null

  numberOfNonProdApps: 4
}
output numberOfApps int = properties.isProd ? properties.
numberOfProdApps : properties.numberOfNonProdApps // 4
...
```

To view the full code snippet, please refer to `Chapter07/ logical.bicep` in this book's GitHub repository.

Now, let's review some numeric operators, which allow you to work with numbers and integers.

Numeric operators

Numeric operators will help you perform all sorts of calculations and return the required value. Here is a list of supported operators:

Symbol	Name	Operand Types	Return Type	Template Equivalent	Description
%	Modulo	`<integer, integer>`	`int`	`mod(v1, v2)`	Calculates the remainder of a division
*	Multiply	`<integer, integer>`	`int`	`mul(v1, v2)`	Multiplies two integers
/	Divide	`<integer, integer>`	`int`	`div(v1, v2)`	Divides two integers
+	Add	`<integer, integer>`	`int`	`add(v1, v2)`	Adds two integers
-	Subtract	`<integer, integer>`	`int`	`sub(v1, v2)`	Subtracts two integers
-	Minus	`int`	`int`	`sub(0, val)`	Multiplies the number by -1

Table 7.3 – Numeric operators

Here are a few examples:

```
// multiply
param firstInt int = 10
var times = 2
output twenty int = firstInt * times // 20


// divide
param numberOfVms int = 10
var storageNeeded = 5
output storagePerVM int = numberOfVms / storageNeeded // 2

...
```

To see all the examples, please visit `Chapter07/numeric.bicep` in this book's GitHub repository.

Not all operators are for calculation or comparison. Sometimes, you will just want to access an element in an array or object. Accessor operators will come to the rescue in those situations, so read on to find out more about them.

Accessor operators

These operators help you access child properties or resources. Let's go through them one by one.

Index accessor

This operator is used with square brackets, `[]`, and its syntax is as follows:

```
array[index]
object['propertyName']
```

You could use this operator to get an item from an array or an object's property. Here is an example:

```
param storageProperties object = {
  storageReplication: 1
}

param supportedReplications array = [
```

```
  'Standard_GRS'
  'Standard_LRS'
]

resource storageaccount 'Microsoft.Storage/
storageAccounts@2021-02-01' = {
  name: 'name'
  location: resourceGroup().location
  kind: 'StorageV2'
  sku: {
    name:
supportedReplications[storageProperties['storageReplication']]
  }
}
```

The preceding code snippet is using a combination of array index and object index to access the replication strategy for the storage account. Next, we'll review function accessors.

Function accessor

Only two functions support the accessor operator – getSecret and list*. Here is an example of using the listKeys function to access the storage account keys:

```
resource stg 'Microsoft.Storage/storageAccounts@2021-02-01' = {
  name: 'name'
  location: resourceGroup().location
  kind: 'StorageV2'
  sku: {
    name: 'Standard_LRS'
  }
}
output storageKey string = stg.listKeys().key[0].value
```

To see an example of getSecret, please visit Chapter07/Accessors/accessor.bicep in this book's GitHub repository.

Sometimes, you want to get a hold of a child resource. For this, you would use a nested accessor.

Nested resource accessor

Let's look at how to use the `parentResource::nestedResource` operator to access a nested resource.

A resource that is defined within a resource is called a **nested resource**. Too many resources, huh? Think of a `blob container` within a storage account; this is a nested resource, and you can access it using this operator.

If you are in the context of the parent resource, you can easily access this nested resource by its symbolic name, but outside of this context, you would use this accessor. Here is an example:

```
resource storage 'Microsoft.Storage/storageAccounts@2021-02-01'
= {
  name: 'examplestorage'
  location: resourceGroup().location
  kind: 'StorageV2'
  sku: {
    name: 'Standard_LRS'
  }

  resource service 'fileServices' = {
    name: 'default'

    resource fileShare 'shares' = {
      name: 'fileshare'
      properties: {
        metadata: {
          parentName: storage.name
        }
      }
    }
  }
}

output fileShareName string = storage::service::fileShare.name
```

Pay attention to the way we used `symbolic name` of the storage account within the file share and how we got access to the file share's name outside of the scope using the accessor operator (: :).

Previously, we saw how to get a hold of an object's property using the index accessor. But there is an easier way to do this: by using the property accessor.

Property accessor

We have used this accessor many times in our previous examples. You simply use a dot (.) to get a value of a property within an object, whether it is a parameter or a resource within your template.

Here is an example that will output the storage account's name:

```
resource storage 'Microsoft.Storage/storageAccounts@2021-02-01'
= {
  name: 'examplestorage'
  location: resourceGroup().location
  kind: 'StorageV2'
  sku: {
    name: 'Standard_LRS'
  }
}
output storageName string = storage.name
```

If you have nested properties within properties, you can nest to the last child property, which you can find in the `Chapter07/Accessors/accessor.bicep` file in this book's GitHub repository.

Now that we have gone through all these operators, it is worth mentioning that these operators can have precedence and associativity. This means that sometimes, the order of usage matters and you need to be aware of how these are interpreted using the compiler.

Operator precedence and associativity

The following table shows the precedence in descending order, which means the higher the position, the higher the precedence:

Symbol	Type of Operation	Associativity
( ) [ ] . ::	Parentheses, array indexers, property indexers, nested resource accessor	Left to right
! -	Unary	Right to left
% * /	Multiplicative	Left to right
+ -	Additive	Left to right
<= < > >=	Relational	Left to right
== != =~ !~	Equality	Left to right
&&	Logical AND	Left to right
||	Logical OR	Left to right
? :	Conditional expression (ternary)	Right to left
??	Coalesce	Left to right

Table 7.4 – The precedence and associativity of operators

To simplify the preceding table, imagine that you have the following operation:

```
output result int = 6 + 10 / 2
```

The preceding result would return 11, which is because / has precedence over +. So, what if you wanted to do the addition first and then division? Looking at the preceding table, you can wrap them in parentheses to give them more priority:

```
output result int = (6 + 10) / 2
```

The preceding code will result in 8. Keep this table in mind when you're writing expressions as this might result in unwanted behavior. Now, let's look at conditions.

Exploring conditions

You have already seen a few examples of using conditions in templates using conditional operators. Conditions can be very beneficial in many different scenarios, whether you want to decide whether a resource should be deployed or not or when calculating a value. But how can we apply these during deployment? That is when deploy conditions come to the rescue.

Deploy condition

You can pass in a parameter or use a variable to decide whether a resource should be deployed or not using this condition. Here is an example:

```
param deployZone bool
resource zone 'Microsoft.Network/dnszones@2018-05-01' = if
(deployZone) {
  name: 'myZone'
  location: 'global'
}
```

Notice the if keyword before the resource definition. This is all you need to enforce your condition during deployment.

New or existing resource

You can also use the same approach to check whether a resource is new or existing during deployment. To achieve this, you can pass a condition in your if statement, as shown in the following code snippet:

```
@allowed([
  'new'
  'existing'
])
param newOrExisting string = 'new'
resource sa 'Microsoft.Storage/storageAccounts@2019-06-01' = if
(newOrExisting == 'new') {
  name: 'storagename'
  location: resourceGroup().location
  sku: {
    name: 'Standard_LRS'
  }
  kind: 'StorageV2'
  properties: {
    accessTier: 'Hot'
  }
}
```

The preceding code snippet will help you choose an existing storage account or create a new one.

Runtime checks

If you conditionally deploy a resource and have a `reference` or `list` function for that resource in your template, you will face an error when the resource does not exist. To avoid this situation, you can use the conditional expression (`? :`):

```
param serverFarmId string = ''


resource azureFunction 'Microsoft.Web/sites@2020-12-01' = if
(!empty(serverFarmId)) {
  name: 'name'
  location: resourceGroup().location
  kind: 'functionapp'
  properties: {
    serverFarmId: ((!empty(serverFarmId)) ?
reference(serverFarmId, '2020-12-01').id : json('null'))
  }
}
```

Notice how we used the `json('null')` function to pass a null value to `serverFarmId` in case the resource is not deployed. This is because `serverFarmId` requires a `null | string` type as a value.

Now that we have gone through all the functions and conditions, it is time to review loops in Bicep.

Diving into resource iterations

Sometimes, you need to create multiple resources of the same type with the same template. Since templates are reusable, it is expected from them to be able to provide the ability to do so. In **Azure Bicep**, you can add loops to resource declarations and dynamically define how many you want to create. Let's learn how this approach can help you avoid repeating syntax within the template.

> **Note**
> Currently, Bicep loops cannot work with negative numbers or go above 800 iterations.

Apart from resource declaration, you can apply loops to `modules`, `properties`, and `outputs`, which you will learn more about in *Chapter 8, Defining Modules and Utilizing Outputs*, of this book. Let's start by looking at syntax.

Syntax

You can use an index in a range to create loops:

```
resource <resource-symbolic-name> '<resource-type>@<api-
version>' = [for <index> in range(<start>, <stop>): {
    <resource-properties>
}]
```

Alternatively, you can use an array:

```
resource <resource-symbolic-name> '<resource-type>@<api-
version>' = [for <item> in <collection>: {
    <resource-properties>
}]
```

Finally, you can mix these two and use arrays and indexes:

```
resource <resource-symbolic-name> '<resource-type>@<api-
version>' = [for (<item>, <index>) in <collection>: {
    <resource-properties>
}]
```

Now, let's look at some examples of these to make them easier to understand.

Loop index

This is the simplest option if you want to create, for example, 10 storage accounts. The index starts at `zero` (`0`) and ends at the `count` parameter you pass into the range function:

```
param storageCount int = 2
param location string = resourceGroup().location
resource storageAcct 'Microsoft.Storage/
storageAccounts@2021-02-01' = [for i in range(0, storageCount):
{
    name: 'storage${i}${uniqueString(resourceGroup().id)}'
```

```
  location: location
  sku: {
    name: 'Standard_LRS'
  }
  kind: 'Storage'
}]
```

Notice how we defined the `location` function outside of the loop. It is always a good practice to *not* call functions in a loop to increase performance. Using an array is another way to create your resources in a loop.

Loop array

If you want your users to pass in some information for each of the resources, you can use an array:

```
param storageNames array = [
  'stg1'
  'stg2'
]


resource storageaccounts 'Microsoft.Storage/
storageAccounts@2021-02-01' = [for name in storageNames: {
  name: name
  location: resourceGroup().location
  kind: 'StorageV2'
  sku: {
    name: 'Premium_LRS'
  }
}]
```

In the preceding example, the user will pass the storage account names for each one to be created.

Loop array and index

You can use an array and index to loop through and create your resources by using its elements. This approach is particularly useful when you want the user of your template to pass in more than how many resources they want; that is, `sku`, `VM size`, and so on:

```
param storageAccountNamePrefix string
var storageConfigurations = [
  {
    suffix: 'local'
    sku: 'Standard_LRS'
  }
  {
    suffix: 'geo'
    sku: 'Standard_GRS'
  }
]

resource storageAccountResources 'Microsoft.Storage/
storageAccounts@2021-02-01' = [for (config, i) in
storageConfigurations: {
  name: '${storageAccountNamePrefix}${config.suffix}${i}'
  location: resourceGroup().location
  properties: {
    supportsHttpsTrafficOnly: true
    accessTier: 'Hot'
  }
  kind: 'StorageV2'
  sku: {
    name: config.sku
  }
}]
```

This is probably the most common use case for loops in IaC that I have seen teams use to create multiple resources.

You can also use nested objects to iterate a resource property.

Nested loops with conditions

The following example that shows how you can use an array with items that have nested properties to create your resources in a loop:

```
var subnets = [
  {
    name: 'web'
    subnetPrefix: '10.20.0.0/24'
  }
  {
    name: 'api'
    subnetPrefix: '10.20.1.0/24'
  }
]
resource vnet 'Microsoft.Network/virtualNetworks@2018-11-01' = {
  name: 'vnet'
  location: resourceGroup().location
  properties: {
    addressSpace: {
      addressPrefixes: [
        '10.20.0.0/20'
      ]
    }
    subnets: [for subnet in subnets: {
      name: subnet.name
      properties: {
        addressPrefix: subnet.subnetPrefix
      }
    }]
  }
}
```

Here, you can see how easy it would be to use a mixture of all the techniques we have reviewed so far to create a very practical, reusable, and maintainable template.

> **Note**
>
> You cannot have a resource within the loop – only properties can be iterated. If you want to iterate child resources, you will need to declare them as top-level resources. An example of this is shown in the `Chapter07/loops.bicep` file in this book's GitHub repository.

You can mix this with conditions to make sure you will not face any issues during deployments. Refer to the `Chapter07/loops.bicep` file in this book's GitHub repository to see an example of this approach. Just keep in mind that the property you would use for the condition should evaluate to a Boolean.

Creating resources in loops can cause side effects, especially if you use multiple CI/CD pipelines that will trigger frequently. This means that many resources would be deployed at the same time, which is not something you want to do. Let's learn how Bicep can help in this situation.

Using batches

If you deploy multiple resources with a loop, **Azure Resource Manager** will create these in parallel by default. With `loops`, there is no guarantee regarding how these resources will be deployed and in what order. If you would like to prevent all of these resources from being created at the same time, you can use the `batchSize` decorator to limit the number of concurrent resource deployments within a loop:

```
param location string = resourceGroup().location
@batchSize(2)
resource storageAccts 'Microsoft.Storage/
storageAccounts@2021-02-01' = [for i in range(0, 4): {
  name: '${i}storage${uniqueString(resourceGroup().id)}'
  location: location
  sku: {
    name: 'Standard_LRS'
  }
  kind: 'Storage'
}]
```

If you want your resources to be deployed completely in order, simply set the `batchSize` value to `1`.

And that is all there is to know about loops and how to use them to create more succinct templates, which can create multiple resources with much less syntax repetition and are easy to read.

Summary

This chapter has been an interesting one to write. We started by reviewing how to write expressions in Bicep with all the different available operators, from comparison to numeric to logical and accessors. Then, we reviewed how to use conditions to deploy our resources conditionally, whether it is just to check whether to deploy the resource or not or checking for an existing resource.

We finished by reviewing different types of loops you can use to take advantage of reusability within your template and create multiple resources without repeating their syntax.

In the next chapter, we will take this discussion even further and review modules to take our reusability to the next level. We will also take a closer look at outputs, although we have used them many times in our examples so far.

8
Defining Modules and Utilizing Outputs

So far, we have looked at many of the different features in Bicep that make it reusable. However, we still have one left to cover: **modules**. In this chapter, we will look at what modules are, as well as how to define and use them in our templates to take reusability to the next level.

We will also introduce outputs and learn what they are used for and how they are constructed. In short, we will cover the following main topics:

- Modules
- Using Bicep outputs

Technical requirements

To take full advantage of this chapter, you will need to have access to a personal computer or laptop that has Visual Studio Code and PowerShell installed. The code for this chapter can be found in this book's GitHub repository at `https://github.com/PacktPublishing/Infrastructure-as-Code-with-Azure-Bicep/tree/main/Chapter08`.

Modules

Similar to **ARM templates**, where you could break down a complex template into a nested template and simplify it, **Azure Bicep** also allows you to do the same using modules. A module in Bicep can contain one or more resources to be deployed together.

Modules help you hide the complexities of raw resource declaration in your main template and put them into separate files, which, in turn, helps with the increased readability in your main templates. This makes it easier to share these modules with other teams in your organization. Let's start by learning how to define modules.

Defining modules

In a sense, every Bicep file can be a module if it has input parameters and outputs that define its contract with the outside world. That said, both parameters and outputs are optional. The following is an example module that deploys a storage account:

```
@minLength(3)
@maxLength(11)
param storagePrefix string

@allowed([
  'Standard_LRS'
  'Premium_LRS'
])
param storageSKU string = 'Standard_LRS'
param location string = resourceGroup().location

var uniqueStorageName =
'${storagePrefix}${uniqueString(resourceGroup().id)}'
```

```
resource stg 'Microsoft.Storage/storageAccounts@2019-04-01' = {
  name: uniqueStorageName
  location: location
  sku: {
    name: storageSKU
  }
  kind: 'StorageV2'
  properties: {
    supportsHttpsTrafficOnly: true
  }
}
output storageEndpoint object = stg.properties.primaryEndpoints
```

The preceding template takes `prefix`, `storage sku`, and `location` properties and then deploys a storage account with those properties. Here, you can see that `sku` has limited options and that `prefix` has validation rules around it, so a module will have full control over what parameters can be passed into it and what should be applied to the resource properties.

But how do we use modules?

Consuming a module

Using a module is as simple as referencing it in your template using a relative path. You need to use the `module` keyword to tell Bicep that this/these resource(s) will be deployed from a separate module:

```
param namePrefix string = 'stg'
param location string = resourceGroup().location
module stgModule './storagemodule.bicep' = {
  name: 'storageDeploy'
  params: {
    storagePrefix: namePrefix
    location: location
  }
}
output storageEndpoint object = stgModule.outputs.
storageEndpoint
```

There are a few things that make this file different from what you have seen so far:

- The `module` keyword.

- `symbolic name`: The module identifier.

- `module file`: The files should be referenced using a relative path to where your template is. All paths should use a forward slash (`/`) as a directory separator; the backslash (`\`) character is not supported. You can have spaces in your paths, which saves you from using encoding or other tricks you must use with other **IaC** providers.

- The `name` property: This is required when you're consuming a module. When you consume your module, this `name` is used to reference the nested deployment resources.

- The `params` property: This is used to pass the required parameters into the module during deployment.

Some features apply to modules as well. Let's review them together.

Additional considerations

By default, modules are deployed in parallel unless you prevent them from using one of the techniques we reviewed previously (such as `implicit` or using `dependsOn`).

You can deploy modules conditionally using the `if` syntax, which you saw in the previous chapter. Here is an example that conditionally deploys our previous storage module:

```
param deployStorage bool
param namePrefix string = 'stg'
param location string = resourceGroup().location
module storageAcc './storagemodule.bicep' = if (deployStorage)
{
  name: 'myZoneModule'
  params: {
    storagePrefix: namePrefix
    location: location
  }
}
```

You can also get outputs from modules, which we will cover later in this chapter.

You can also use loops with modules to deploy a module multiple times using either `index`, `array`, or the `array` and `index` approach, which we reviewed in the previous chapter. Here is an example of using `array` to create a module within an iteration:

```
param location string = resourceGroup().location
param storageAccArray array = [
  {
    name: 'stgDeployment1'
    prefix: 'stg1'
  }
  {
    name: 'stgDeployment2'
    prefix: 'stg2'
  }
]
module storageAccs './storagemodule.bicep' = [for stg in
storageAccArray: {
  name: stg.name
  params: {
    storagePrefix: stg.prefix
    location: location
  }
}]
```

For more examples, please refer to `Chapter08/loops.bicep` in this book's GitHub repository. Conditionally deploying modules in a loop is also supported, similar to resources using the `if` syntax.

Now, it is time to review what scopes can be supplied to a module during deployment.

Defining and configuring module scopes

You can deploy modules across several scopes using the scope property when you are declaring your module. Here is an example of deploying our storage module in a different resource group:

```
param namePrefix string = 'stg'
param scopeLocation string
param resourceGroupName string
module scopedMod './storagemodule.bicep' = {
  name: 'myScopedModule'
  scope: resourceGroup(resourceGroupName)
  params: {
    storagePrefix: namePrefix
    location: scopeLocation
  }
}
```

You can skip the scope property if you intend to deploy it in the same scope as your parent file. Here, you can have a Bicep file with a subscription scope and then deploy your modules in a resource group within that subscription. Here is an example of this approach:

```
targetScope = 'subscription'
param location string = deployment().location
resource myResourceGroup 'Microsoft.Resources/
resourceGroups@2020-01-01' = {
  name: 'moduleRG'
  location: location
  scope: subscription()
}
module stgModule './storagemodule.bicep' = {
  name: 'storageDeploy'
  scope: myResourceGroup
  params: {
    storagePrefix: 'stg'
    location: location
  }
}
```

Notice how we used the `myResourceGroup` symbolic name as a scope for the storage account module. This is because if you are deploying in multiple scopes and one of the resources is created within the same template, it makes it a valid scope for sub-resources.

Just keep in mind that you can only have `tenant`, `management group`, `subscription`, and `resource group` satisfying this rule.

And that was everything you needed to know about modules. Now that we have mentioned outputs a few times, let's review them.

Using Bicep outputs

Outputs have been an essential part of **ARM templates** and remain the same for Bicep. Regardless of what you are deploying, there will be many scenarios where you need to pass a property, name, connection string, or any other information to be used later. This will be more important in cases where the deployment is happening as part of a **CI/CD** pipeline, and you have a dependency on one of the resources that's being deployed using Bicep.

Outputs will need to have a type, which we learned about earlier in this book. Now, let's learn how to define outputs.

Defining outputs

Outputs are in the following format:

```
output <name> <type> = <value>
```

The `output` keyword is what makes this line a form of output in Bicep. It needs to be followed by a name and type and then be assigned a value. This value can be from any of the resource properties or even a variable or parameter that has been passed in. The following code block shows how to output the fully qualified domain name of a public IP address:

```
resource pip 'Microsoft.Network/publicIPAddresses@2019-11-01' =
{
  name: 'name'
  location: resourceGroup().location
  properties: {
    publicIPAllocationMethod: 'Dynamic'
    dnsSettings: {
      domainNameLabel: 'dnsname'
    }
```

```
    }
}
output fqdn string = pip.properties.dnsSettings.fqdn
```

As we mentioned earlier, you can output a parameter or variable, as well as resource properties. You will need to use the property accessor (.) to access the intended property.

If you have a property or a name that has a dash/hyphen (-) in its name, do not use the property accessor. Instead, use brackets ([ ]). Take a look at the following example to understand this implication:

```
param storageProps object = {
    'storage-name': 'myStorageName'
}
output storageName string = storageProps['storage-name']
```

You can also use functions to get the value you need to output. The following example shows different types of outputs:

```
output location string = resourceGroup().location
output rgTags int = length(resourceGroup().tags)
output isProd bool = environment().name == 'prod'
output audiences array = environment().authentication.audiences
output sub object = subscription()
```

You can also return outputs conditionally. Read on to find out how.

Conditional outputs

Generally, you would not return a value conditionally unless you have a conditionally deployed resource. You can use the condition operator (?) to achieve this:

```
param shouldDeploy bool = false
resource publicIP 'Microsoft.Network/
publicIPAddresses@2019-11-01' = if (shouldDeploy) {
    name: 'pip'
    location: resourceGroup().location
}
output domainName string = shouldDeploy ? publicIP.properties.
dnsSettings.fqdn : ''
```

If you have a loop within your template, you can reuse the same technique to output the resource properties that get created as part of that instead of repeating them one by one.

Returning multiple outputs with loops

Sometimes, you have a loop and will be creating multiple resources in an iteration. You can use the same technique to return multiple outputs from those resources. Here is an example showcasing how to do so:

```
param pipLoction string = resourceGroup().location
param publicIPs array = [
  'pip1'
  'pip2'
  'pip3'
]
resource publicIPAdds 'Microsoft.Network/
publicIPAddresses@2019-11-01' = [for name in publicIPs: {
  name: name
  location: pipLoction
  properties: {
    dnsSettings: {
      domainNameLabel: name
    }
  }
}]
output fqdns array = [for (name, i) in publicIPs: {
  name: publicIPs[i]
  fqdn: publicIPAdds[i].properties.dnsSettings.fqdn
}]
```

As we mentioned previously, you can output the output of a module you have just deployed.

Module outputs

If you are deploying a module and you want to output the output of the deployed module, you can simply access the `output` property of its symbolic name:

```
param stgLocation string = resourceGroup().location

module stgAcc './storagemodule.bicep' = {
  name: 'stgModule'
  params: {
    location: stgLocation
    storagePrefix: 'stg'
    storageSKU: 'Standard_LRS'
  }
}
output storageEndpoint object = stgAcc.outputs.storageEndpoint
```

Not only can you output the module outputs, but also use them within your template to populate properties of resources that have dependencies on the deployed module. You can find an example of this in the `Chapter08/ouput.bicep` file in this book's GitHub repository.

Now, there is only one thing left to cover, which is how to get access to the deployment outputs from outside.

Getting output values after deployment

If you have a completed deployment and wanted to access its outputs, you can do so using the **Azure CLI** or **Azure PowerShell**. The following code block shows the command you need to run using the Azure CLI to retrieve the outputs:

```
az deployment group show \
  -g <resource-group-name> \
  -n <deployment-name> \
  --query properties.outputs.resourceID.value
```

The following does the same job but via Azure PowerShell:

```
(Get-AzResourceGroupDeployment `
    -ResourceGroupName <resource-group-name> `
    -Name <deployment-name>).Outputs.resourceID.value
```

> **Note**
> For subscription, management group, or tenant-level deployments, you will need to use their commands, that is, `az deployment sub show` or `az deployment mg show`.

Keep in mind that you must have the deployment name to be able to retrieve the properties after the deployment. The alternative is to use the `list` command instead of `show` and find the one you are looking for by iterating through the result. Hopefully, this section has provided some insights into how to return values from your templates.

Summary

In this chapter, we learned how to define modules and how useful they can be to create more readable, simpler, and reusable templates with Bicep. We reviewed how to define and consume modules and some of the tips you need to be aware of when using them.

Then, we officially covered outputs and learned how to return values or properties to the outside world, how to conditionally return a value, how to return them via a loop, and then reviewed the module outputs. This chapter concludes all the topics you need to know about Bicep to be able to create templates.

In the next chapter, we will review the different ways of deploying them, so get ready for some action!

Section 3: Deploying Azure Bicep Templates

In this section, you will learn how to deploy your templates locally using CI/CD tools such as GitHub Actions or Azure DevOps.

This part of the book comprises the following chapters:

- *Chapter 9, Deploying a Local Template*
- *Chapter 10, Deploying Bicep Using Azure DevOps*
- *Chapter 11, Deploying Bicep Templates Using GitHub Actions*
- *Chapter 12, Exploring Best Practices for Future Maintenance*

9
Deploying a Local Template

Now that you have learned all about Bicep and its mechanics, it is time to learn how to deploy your templates. For you to be confident about your templates and their results, you need to test them locally and make sure there are no errors or warnings that might cause trouble later during the deployment.

In this chapter, you will learn how to compile your Bicep files, test your deployment without deploying the template, and how to deal with potential warnings and errors. Once you have finished reading this chapter, you will be able to commit your templates into your source code repository with confidence, ready for deployment. You will also know how to deal with possible issues before and during deployment.

In this chapter, we are going to cover the following main topics:

- Deploying Bicep with Azure PowerShell
- Deploying Bicep with the Azure CLI
- Troubleshooting potential warnings and errors

Technical requirements

To take full advantage of this chapter, you will need to have access to a personal computer or laptop that has Visual Studio Code and PowerShell installed. The code for this chapter can be found in this book's GitHub repository at `https://github.com/PacktPublishing/Infrastructure-as-Code-with-Azure-Bicep/tree/main/Chapter09`.

Deploying Bicep with Azure PowerShell

As we mentioned in *Chapter 2*, *Installing Azure Bicep*, for you to be able to deploy Bicep files using **Azure PowerShell**, you need to have version 5.6.0 or later installed. Once you have your Bicep file ready to be deployed, open a PowerShell terminal (it is not important whether you use the integrated terminal in VS Code or an independent one). Once done, you need to log into Azure first.

Connecting to your Azure environment

You will need to use the `Connect-AzAccount` command to log into Azure:

```
Connect-AzAccount
```

This will open a browser window where you get to log into your Azure tenant. Once you've done this, it will pass the authenticated context back to your terminal:

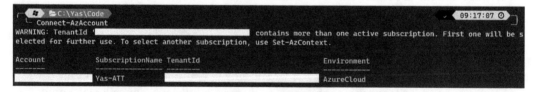

Figure 9.1 – Connecting to Azure using Azure PowerShell

If you have access to multiple subscriptions in your tenant, you will see a message similar to the previous one, where you will need to use the `Set-AzContext` command to select your desired subscription.

Once authenticated, you will be ready to start your local test and deployment. Before you deploy your template, you can test it using the `what-if` operation. So, let's review that next.

Previewing changes with the what-if operation

As you may have noticed, I have not mentioned anything about compiling your templates so far, and that is because both the Azure CLI and Azure PowerShell have built-in integration with Bicep, which means they will take care of the compilation for you behind the scenes. You will use the `New-AzResourceGroupDeployment` command to deploy Bicep, so you need to pass the `-Whatif` flag to this command:

```
New-AzResourceGroupDeployment -TemplateFile ./main.bicep
 -ResourceGroupName Bicep -Whatif
```

If you do not have any errors in your template and everything can be deployed successfully, you will get a message similar to the following:

Figure 9.2 – Using the what-if operation

Now that your template can be deployed successfully, you can go ahead and deploy it by removing the `-Whatif` flag in the command. You can find the file we used for the preceding example in `Chapter09/main.bicep`, in this book's GitHub repository.

In many cases, you will need to pass parameters to your Bicep files. Let's explore how that is done.

Passing parameters

You can pass your parameters inline or in a parameter file. In the inline approach, you pass your parameters in a similar way to how you did with ARM templates:

```
New-AzResourceGroupDeployment -ResourceGroupName Bicep `
  -TemplateFile main.bicep `
  -namePrefix mystg `
  -location australiaeast `
  -sku 'Standard_LRS'
```

If you have done everything right, you should see a success message for your deployment, like so:

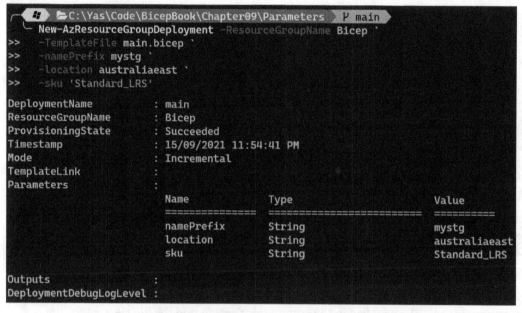

Figure 9.3 – Using inline parameters with Azure PowerShell

The template that was used for this command is located at Chapter09/Parameters/ main.bicep in this book's GitHub repository.

If you wanted to pass a parameter file, you can use the same parameter file structure you use for your ARM templates and pass it using the -TemplateParameterFile parameter:

```
New-AzResourceGroupDeployment -ResourceGroupName Bicep `
  -TemplateFile main.bicep `
  -TemplateParameterFile main.parameters.json
```

Bicep does not have a parameter file structure, which is why we must use the good old ARM template style file for deployment. You can find the parameter file in the same folder as the Bicep file.

There are other possibilities as well, such as reading a file and passing its content as a parameter, like so:

```
New-AzResourceGroupDeployment -ResourceGroupName Bicep `
  -TemplateFile main.bicep `
  -namePrefix mystg `
  -location australiaeast `
  -sku $(Get-Content -Path sku.txt -Raw)
```

So far, we have used a local Bicep file, but if you want to use a remote file, you will need to compile it to JSON first using the Bicep CLI or the Azure CLI, then upload it to the remote location and deploy it, as you have been doing with ARM templates.

All our examples have been targeting resource groups, but if yours is going to be deployed into management groups, subscriptions, or even the tenant, then you must use the appropriate command from Azure PowerShell.

Deployment scopes

If your template is targeting a subscription, then you need to use the `New-AzSubscriptionDeployment` command:

```
New-AzSubscriptionDeployment -Location <location> -TemplateFile
<path-to-bicep>
```

Similarly, if you are targeting a management group, then you need to use the `New-AzManagementGroupDeployment` command:

```
New-AzManagementGroupDeployment -ManagementGroupId <management-
group-id> -Location <location> -TemplateFile <path-to-bicep>
```

Finally, if you are targeting the tenant, use the `New-AzTenantDeployment` command:

```
New-AzTenantDeployment -Location <location> -TemplateFile
<path-to-bicep>
```

Keep in mind that not all resources can be deployed in each scope. For more information about what can or cannot be deployed, please visit `https://docs.microsoft.com/en-us/azure/azure-resource-manager/bicep/deploy-to-resource-group?tabs=azure-powershell`.

Apart from your Bicep files, you can also deploy template specs. However, Azure PowerShell does not support this via Bicep files. You can create your template specs by using the `Microsoft.Resources/templateSpecs` namespace in a Bicep file. To see an example of this, visit `https://github.com/Azure/azure-docs-bicep-samples/blob/main/samples/create-template-spec/azuredeploy.bicep`.

The last thing worth pointing out is that you can set a name for your deployments, regardless of what scope you are using. By default, if you do not provide a name, it will use the filename, so make sure that you provide a name if you intend to find the deployment or use its outputs later:

```
$suffix = Get-Random -Maximum 1000
$deploymentName = "MyDeployment" + $suffix
New-AzResourceGroupDeployment `
  -Name $deploymentName `
  -ResourceGroupName Bicep `
  -TemplateFile main.bicep
```

To ensure you do not run into any issues with concurrent deployments or find your deployments easier, make sure you give them a unique name. Now that you have learned how to validate and deploy your Bicep files with Azure PowerShell, let's learn how to do the same via the Azure CLI.

Deploying Bicep with the Azure CLI

The procedure is the same with the **Azure CLI**, so let's review the necessary commands to validate and deploy our Bicep files with this cross-platform CLI.

The first thing you should know – and it has been pointed out before – is that you need to have version **2.20.0** or later of the Azure CLI installed. Once you have installed it, you need to log in and connect to your Azure environment.

Connecting to your Azure environment

All the Azure CLI commands will begin with the `az` keyword. To log in, simply run the following command:

```
az login
```

A browser window will appear where you can log in. Once you have done this, it will pass the authenticated context to your terminal. If you have multiple subscriptions, as we did with Azure PowerShell, use the `az account` command:

```
az account set -s <subscriptionid or name>
```

Now, you are ready to deploy your Bicep files. The Azure CLI also has built-in integration with Bicep, so if you have any compilation errors, it will point them out. We will review these in the last section, where we will review the troubleshooting steps. You will probably start by validating your deployment with the `what-if` operation.

Preview changes with what-if operation

As we did with Azure PowerShell, you can use the `what-if` flag to validate your template without deploying it:

```
az deployment group what-if `
    --resource-group Bicep `
    --template-file main.bicep
```

If everything is in order, you will see the following output:

```
Resource and property changes are indicated with this symbol:
  + Create

The deployment will update the following scope:

Scope: /subscriptions/                              /resourceGroups/Bicep

  + Microsoft.Storage/storageAccounts/stgreopd7q6wravw [2021-02-01]

      apiVersion: "2021-02-01"
      id:         "/subscriptions                              /resourceGroups/Bicep/providers/Microsoft
.Storage/storageAccounts/stgreopd7q6wravw"
      kind:       "StorageV2"
      location:   "australiaeast"
      name:       "stgreopd7q6wravw"
      sku.name:   "Premium_LRS"
      type:       "Microsoft.Storage/storageAccounts"

Resource changes: 1 to create.
```

Figure 9.4 – Previewing the changes with the Azure CLI using the what-if operation

You can find the file that was used for this example in `Chapter09/main.bicep` in this book's GitHub repository. Once you are happy with the result, you can replace `what-if` with `create` and deploy your template:

```
az deployment group create `
  --resource-group Bicep `
  --template-file main.bicep
```

Now, let's learn how to pass parameters to Azure CLI commands.

Passing parameters

You can pass parameters to **Azure CLI** commands as well, both inline and through parameter files. To pass inline parameters, you need to make a slight adjustment, similar to what we did with Azure PowerShell:

```
az deployment group create `
  --resource-group Bicep `
  --template-file main.bicep `
  --parameters location=australiaeast namePrefix=stg
sku=Standard_LRS
```

You should see the result of your deployment shortly after. You can pass the content of a file as the value of your parameter:

```
az deployment group create `
  --resource-group Bicep `
  --template-file main.bicep `
  --parameters location=australiaeast namePrefix=stg sku=$(Get-
Content -Path sku.txt -Raw)
```

If you are using a Bash terminal, this will be even easier as you just need to add an @ symbol at the beginning of the filename:

```
az deployment group create \
  --resource-group Bicep \
  --template-file main.bicep \
  --parameters location=australiaeast namePrefix=stg sku=@sku.
txt
```

Note that if you are using Bash, you can pass a JSON string as a parameter value, as follows:

```
tags='{"Owner":"myDept","Cost Center":"2345-324"}'
```

However, if you are using a PowerShell-based terminal, you need to escape the quotation marks, like so:

```
$tags = '{\"Owner\":\"myDept\",\"Cost Center\":\"2345-324\"}'
```

You can also pass parameter files instead of providing the parameters one by one:

```
az deployment group create `
    --resource-group Bicep `
    --template-file main.bicep `
    --parameter main.parameters.json
```

This parameter file is the same one we used earlier and can be found in `Chapter09/Parameters/main.parameters.json` in this book's GitHub repository.

The Azure CLI also does not support remote Bicep files. Therefore, you will need to compile to JSON first, upload it somewhere, and then deploy it using the Azure CLI. To find out how to deploy a remote ARM template, visit the documentation at `https://docs.microsoft.com/en-us/azure/azure-resource-manager/templates/deploy-cli#deploy-remote-template`.

Again, all our examples have been targeting resource groups, so let's review the other scopes as well.

Deployment scopes

If you are targeting a subscription, you will need to use the following command instead:

```
az deployment sub create --location <location> --template-file
<path-to-bicep>
```

For management groups, you can use the following command:

```
az deployment mg create --location <location> --template-file
<path-to-bicep>
```

For tenant deployments, you can use the following command:

```
az deployment tenant create --location <location> --template-
file <path-to-bicep>
```

Remember that the user who is deploying these resources should have the corresponding permissions. The resources should be compatible with those scopes.

The Azure CLI does not support template specs either. You can create your template specs with the `Microsoft.Resources/templateSpecs` namespace in a Bicep file. To see an example of this, please visit `https://github.com/Azure/azure-docs-bicep-samples/blob/main/samples/create-template-spec/azuredeploy.bicep`.

Finally, you should follow the same rules when it comes to giving your deployments a name. You can pass the name to your Azure CLI commands using the `--name` parameter:

```
deploymentName='mydeployment'$RANDOM\
az deployment group create \
   --name $deploymentName \
   --resource-group Bicep \
   --template-file main.bicep \
```

And that is all you need to know to be able to validate and deploy your Bicep files using the Azure CLI. However, not all validations and deployments are without error. Now, it's time to review some common issues and learn how to resolve them.

Troubleshooting possible errors and warnings

Every time you try to validate or deploy your Bicep files, you might face a compile or deploy time issue. We start with compile issues and then move on to deployment time potential errors.

Compile-time errors and warnings

Depending on what type of linting rules you have, you might receive different errors or warnings. We do not need to cover linting errors since they are obvious. But if you have any linting configuration within your code repository, the tools will give you the rule name when failing the compilation or deployment.

Apart from that, some compile-time errors may occur because of missing properties, the wrong value being provided to a parameter, missing parameters, and more. You will receive these errors, along with the exact locations of where they are happening, which makes them easier to fix. Here is an example of what happens when you do not provide a required property:

```
#  C:\Yas\Code\BicepBook\Chapter09\CompileIssues   ʮ main                         ✓  19:08:37 ⏱
     az deployment group create -g Bicep --template-file main.bicep
C:\Yas\Code\BicepBook\Chapter09\CompileIssues\main.bicep(1,10) : Error BCP035: The specified "resource"
declaration is missing the following required properties: "name".
```

Figure 9.5 – Compile-time errors when a property is missing

You can find this file within the `Chapter09/CompileIssues` folder in this book's GitHub repository.

Many errors might occur during the deployment. So, let's review some of them.

Deployment-time errors

You may come across a situation where you have done everything right but you are still receiving an error. These errors might be occurring because of reasons outside of your control. Therefore, you need to know about them and the steps you can take to resolve them. One of the common ones is when you do not have the necessary resource provider registered in your subscription.

No registered provider

This error occurs when you do not have the resource provider registered in your subscription for one of the resources in your template. If you are not familiar with the concept of resource providers, please visit `https://docs.microsoft.com/en-us/azure/azure-resource-manager/management/resource-providers-and-types`.

```
Code: NoRegisteredProviderFound
Message: No registered resource provider found for location
{location}
and API version {api-version} for type {resource-type}.
```

If you face this error, simply register the provider mentioned in `{resource-type}` of your subscription. Currently, when you deploy the resource and have the necessary permissions to register the provider, it will happen automatically, and you will not receive an error.

Deployment quota exceeded

This error occurs when you have reached the limit of 800 deployments in your deployment history, and you have opted out of automatic deletion. This will happen to teams that do continuous deployments via CI/CD pipelines and commit multiple times a day. To resolve this, simply delete some of the previous deployments.

You can use the following command to delete all the deployments from the last 10 days:

```
startdate=$(date +%F -d "-10days")
deployments=$(az deployment group list --resource-group
exampleGroup --query "[?properties.timestamp<'$startdate'].
name" --output tsv)
for deployment in $deployments
do
   az deployment group delete --resource-group exampleGroup
--name $deployment
done
```

Once the code has finished running, you can rerun your deployment. This time, it should be successful.

Resource not found

This error occurs when you have referenced an existing resource in your template as a dependency, but the resource does not exist. You can find an example Bicep file in the `Chapter09/MissingDependency` folder in this book's GitHub repository:

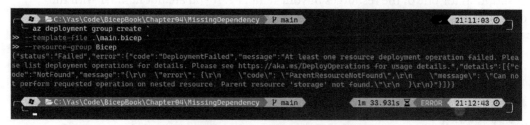

Figure 9.6 – Resource not found error

To resolve this error, make sure you are referencing the correct resource and that it exists in the specified resource group.

Request disallowed by policy

Sometimes, your organization will apply some policies to streamline the deployment processes and prevent a specific resource from being created in the entire tenant. In this case, when you try to perform a deployment, the policy will prevent it from happening and you will get an error that's similar to the following:

```
{
    "statusCode": "Forbidden",
    "serviceRequestId": null,
    "statusMessage": "{\"error\":{\"code\":\"RequestDisallowedBy-
Policy\",\"message\":\"The resource action 'Microsoft.Network/
publicIpAddresses/write' is disallowed by one or more poli-
cies. Policy identifier(s): '/subscriptions/{guid}/providers/
Microsoft.Authorization/policyDefinitions/regionPolicyDefini-
tion'.\"}}",
    "responseBody": "{\"error\":{\"code\":\"RequestDisallowedBy-
Policy\",\"message\":\"The resource action 'Microsoft.Network/
publicIpAddresses/write' is disallowed by one or more poli-
cies. Policy identifier(s): '/subscriptions/{guid}/providers/
Microsoft.Authorization/policyDefinitions/regionPolicyDefini-
tion'.\"}}"
}
```

To resolve this error, you do not have any choice but to contact your administrators and find out whether you are allowed to deploy your resource and if so, what steps you should take.

Reserved resource name

There are quite a few reserved words that you cannot choose for your resource names. These might be trademarks or reserved words by Microsoft. Here are some examples:

- Access
- Azure
- Bing
- Bizspark
- Biztalk
- Cortana

If you try to deploy a resource with any of these names, you will face an error, as shown in the following screenshot:

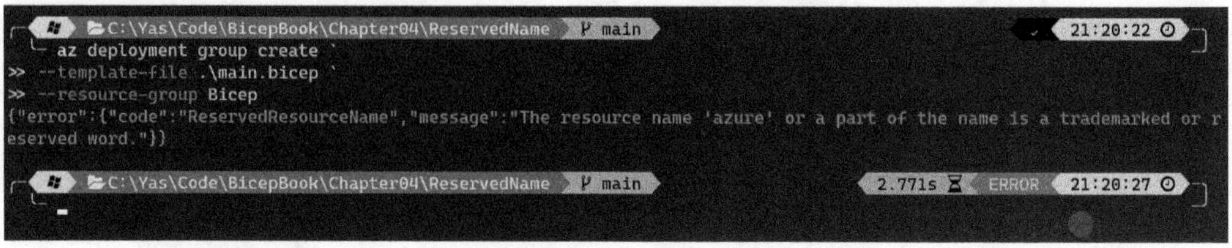

Figure 9.7 – Reserved word error

You can find this file in the Chapter09/ReservedName folder in this book's GitHub repository.

Parent resource not found

If you are deploying a child resource and have not got the correct reference for the parent, you might face this error:

```
Code=ParentResourceNotFound;
Message=Can not perform requested operation on nested resource.
Parent resource 'mysqlserver' not found."
```

This error might also occur if the resource and its parent are not in the same resource group (for those resources where this is a requirement) or the child resource is not in the correct format.

Resource quota exceeded

If you deploy resources that exceed your quota, you will receive this error:

```
Code=ResourceQuotaExceeded
Message=Creating the resource of type <resource-type> would
exceed the quota of <number>
resources of type <resource-type> per resource group. The
current resource count is <number>,
please delete some resources of this type before creating a new
one.
```

If it is related to **virtual machines (VMs)** and vCPUs, you might see an error that's similar to the following:

```
Code=OperationNotAllowed
Message=Operation results in exceeding quota limits of Core.
Maximum allowed: <number>, Current in use: <in use>, Additional
requested: <requested number>.
```

To fix these types of errors, you have a few options. First and foremost, you can request a limit increase by raising a support ticket to Microsoft. You can find this in the subscription blade, within the **Usage + quotas** menu:

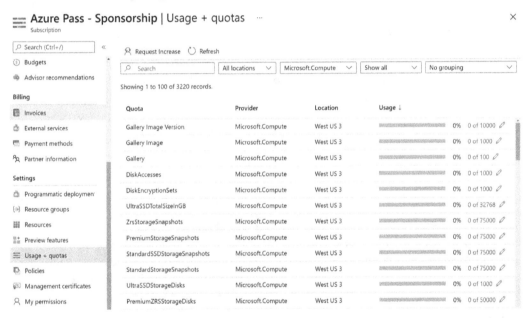

Figure 9.8 – Requesting an increase regarding the resource quota

If, for some reason, your request could not be resolved, you might have to use a different location or a different subscription to deploy your resources.

Finally, it is usually a good practice to investigate the current resources and remove what is not needed so that you don't face this error in the first place. There have been many scenarios where developers have created resources and forgotten about them. Not everything is about cost. Sometimes, keeping the quota free would help other teams within the organization perform their tasks without having to go through all the hassle.

SKU is not available

If you are deploying a resource, especially a virtual machine, you might face this error if Azure cannot find the specified SKU in that region/zone or an alternative one. In this case, you have the option to request an SKU by creating a new support ticket or choosing an available SKU:

```
Code: SkuNotAvailable
Message: The requested tier for resource '<resource>' is
currently not available in location '<location>'
for subscription '<subscriptionID>'. Please try another tier or
deploy to a different location.
```

You can find out which regions have your required SKU by running the following command using Azure PowerShell:

```
Get-AzComputeResourceSku | where {$_.Locations -icontains
"location_name"}
```

Just replace location_name with your region name and you are good to go. Keep in mind that you might receive a NotAvailableForSubscription error if the SKU is not available in that region.

Job size exceeded

If you receive this error, it might indicate that one of the limitations of your deployment has been exceeded. It might be that the template is too large, or the job is too big. Any deployment job can have a maximum size of 1 MB, which includes the metadata about the request. If your template is too large, it can go beyond that, combined with the job's size.

Your templates cannot go beyond 4 MB in size, which is calculated after every expression is translated, such as loops or any value calculation. There are some other limitations as well, as follows:

- Maximum of 256 parameters
- Maximum of 256 variables
- Maximum of 800 resources within the template
- Maximum of 64 output values
- Maximum of 24,567 characters in the template

There are a few ways you can fix these types of issues. First, try to simplify your templates or break them down into linked templates. Divide your resources into logical groups and deploy them into separate resource groups with templates. To be honest, if you have around 800 resources in your template, I would love to have a conversation with you to understand your needs better.

The second solution is to shorten the names of parameters, variables, outputs, and so on. This does not have the same effect as our first solution; however, it can play a small role in getting the errors resolved.

Other errors

There are other errors you might face that go beyond the scope of this book. You can find out more about them at `https://docs.microsoft.com/en-us/azure/azure-resource-manager/templates/common-deployment-errors`.

And that concludes this section of this chapter. Reviewing all these errors will help you know what steps to take when it comes to troubleshooting possible issues you might face before and during deployments, which, in turn, increases your efficiency.

Summary

This chapter was the start of your journey once you have written your templates and they are ready to be deployed. We reviewed how to validate and deploy your templates with the Azure CLI and Azure PowerShell from your local development environment. We also looked at some common compile-time and runtime errors and how to resolve them. Hopefully, this chapter has helped you start testing your templates locally and identifying the causes of any possible issues you might face pre or post-deployment. This chapter should have also increased your confidence in your templates so that you can commit them, along with the rest of the code, if you have **Infrastructure as Code** (**IaC**) in place.

In the next chapter, we will go beyond local deployment and delve into deploying our templates as part of **CI/CD** pipelines.

10

Deploying Bicep Using Azure DevOps

You now know how to validate and deploy your templates from your local environment, which is great. However, you should now commit your templates into your source control repository to be able to implement your **Infrastructure as Code (IaC)** pipeline. There are many tools out there that can help you implement a continuous integration and continuous delivery pipeline, but Microsoft has the advantage of having two very strong tools you can use: **Azure Pipelines** and **GitHub actions**.

In this chapter, we will review how to get started with Azure Pipelines and deploy your Bicep files to create your environment. Then, you will deploy your code in that environment.

In this chapter, we are going to cover the following main topics:

- Creating the Azure DevOps pipeline
- Adding validation steps to your pipeline
- Adding deployment steps to your pipeline
- Accessing the deployment outputs in your pipeline

Technical requirements

To take full advantage of this chapter, you will need to have access to a personal computer or laptop that has Visual Studio Code, the Azure CLI or Azure PowerShell, and Git installed. The code for this chapter is stored in this book's GitHub repository at `https://github.com/PacktPublishing/Infrastructure-as-Code-with-Azure-Bicep/tree/main/Chapter10`.

Creating the Azure DevOps pipeline

Azure DevOps is a suite of products that helps organizations with their projects and DevOps practices. You can sign up for free at `https://azure.microsoft.com/en-us/services/devops/?nav=min`. If you already have access to an organization, use that for this chapter. To follow along with this chapter, you will need to complete a few prerequisites steps. So, let's go through them first.

Prerequisites

As I mentioned earlier, you need an Azure DevOps organization, so create one if you do not have access to it already (use the steps at `https://docs.microsoft.com/en-us/azure/devops/organizations/accounts/create-organization?view=azure-devops` to create an organization and a project within that if you are not familiar with this process already). Make sure you have the **project administrator** role in the project you intend to use for this chapter.

Next, you need to have a service connection between Azure DevOps and the Azure environment where you will be deploying your resources. This service connection is used by your deployment steps and permits them to run commands to deploy resources in your Azure subscription. You can find the instructions on how to create one at `https://docs.microsoft.com/en-us/azure/devops/pipelines/library/connect-to-azure?view=azure-devops`.

Once you have done all this, you need to push the code to the project's GitHub repository. You can find the instructions for this in the following snippet, which is also listed on the repository's default page:

```
git remote add origin https://bicepbook@dev.azure.com/
bicepbook/Bicep/_git/Bicep
git push -u origin --all
```

The URL will be different for you based on the organization and project name you have chosen. Other than that, everything else should be good for you to get started.

The next step is to create your pipeline. I have added a basic pipeline for you to use and follow along with, which looks like this:

```
trigger:
  - main
name: Deploy Bicep files
variables:
  vmImageName: "ubuntu-latest"
pool:
  vmImage: $(vmImageName)
steps:
- task: Bash@3
  inputs:
    targetType: "inline"
    script: |
      # Write your commands here
      echo 'Hello world'
```

The preceding pipeline runs a Linux-based job and prints a `Hello world` message, which is enough to let you create a pipeline in Azure DevOps from an existing YAML file.

Creating a pipeline in Azure DevOps

Once you have the files in the `Chapter10` folder in your GitHub repository, go ahead and click on the **Pipelines** menu on the left-hand side, as shown in the following screenshot:

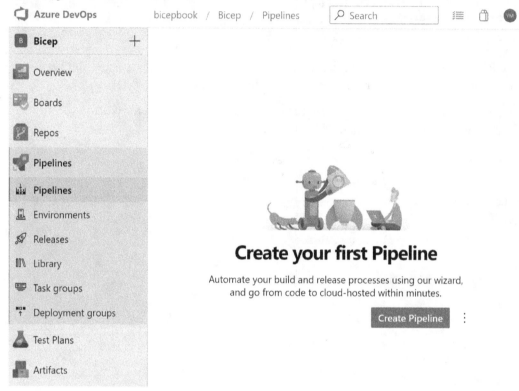

Figure 10.1 – Adding a pipeline in Azure DevOps

Once the page has loaded, click on the **Create Pipeline** button and select the first option (**Azure Repo Git - YAML**). Select your repository when it is shown and choose the **Existing Azure Pipeline YAML file** option:

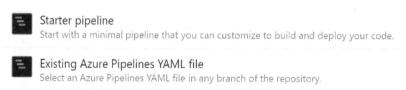

Figure 10.2 – Creating a pipeline from an existing YAML file

You should see a pop-up at this point, asking you to select your branch, which is main in our case, and the path to your YAML file. Go ahead and choose the infra.yml file located in the repository:

Select an existing YAML file   ✕

Select an Azure Pipelines YAML file in any branch of the repository.

Branch

⎇ main   ⌄

Path

/infra.yml   ⌄

Select a file from the dropdown or type in the path to your file

Bicep ⧉

Figure 10.3 – Selecting the existing YAML file for the pipeline

Now, click on the **Run** button on the right-hand side to save your pipeline and run it. You should see the job succeed and a screen similar to the following:

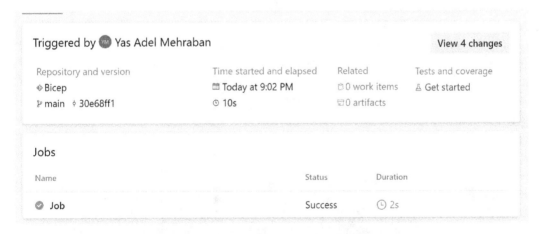

Triggered by 🔵 Yas Adel Mehraban			View 4 changes
Repository and version	Time started and elapsed	Related	Tests and coverage
◈ Bicep	🗓 Today at 9:02 PM	🗂 0 work items	⚄ Get started
⌥ main ◈ 30e68ff1	⊘ 10s	⊜ 0 artifacts	

Jobs

Name	Status	Duration
✔ Job	Success	🕒 2s

Figure 10.4 – Azure Pipeline job run successfully

Of course, we have not added any steps here to either validate or deploy our template, but this will make us ready to go ahead and add those since we now have a working pipeline in place.

Adding a validation step to our pipeline

Now that we have a fully working pipeline, we should be ready to add the necessary steps to validate and deploy our template. However, first, we need a few variables in our YAML file. Go ahead and add the following variables under the `vmImageName` variable, which you can do either by editing the code locally using VS Code or directly in the Azure DevOps portal:

```
azureServiceConnection: "AzureDevOpsConnection"
resourceGroupName: "Bicep"
location: "australiaeast"
templateFile: "./main.bicep"
```

Remember that you need to have completed the prerequisite steps and have the service connection at the subscription level created. If the name of your connection is different, simply update the value before adding it to your YAML file. Also, feel free to update your resource group name and location if you wish. Now is the time to add our validation step.

Validating the deployment

Before we add our validation step, we should make sure that we have created our resource group. Remove the current step in the YAML file and add the following code:

```
- task: AzureCLI@2
  inputs:
    azureSubscription: $(azureServiceConnection)
    scriptType: bash
    scriptLocation: inlineScript
    inlineScript: |
      az group create --name $(resourceGroupName) --location $(location)
```

Since YAML is indent-sensitive, make sure you get those right. You can use an extension in VS Code such as `docs-yaml` from Microsoft or YAML from RedHat:

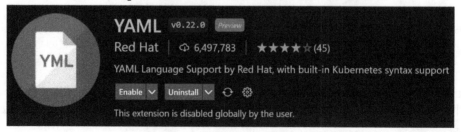

Figure 10.5 – YAML extension in VS Code

Next, we need to add our validation step. This step is optional, but I see a great benefit here, which is to get any errors or potential issues without deploying any resources. Add another step to use the `what-if` operation using the following code snippet:

```
- task: AzureCLI@2
  displayName: Validate deployment
  inputs:
    azureSubscription: $(azureServiceConnection)
    scriptType: bash
    scriptLocation: inlineScript
    inlineScript: |
      az deployment group what-if --resource-group
$(resourceGroupName) --template-file $(templateFile)
```

Now, we need to add our changes, commit our code, and push it to our Azure repo. You can do so by running the following commands:

```
git add .
git commit -m "Added validation steps"
git push
```

Your pipeline should trigger automatically. After the execution is completed, you should see a success message. You can also have a look at the detailed logs for your pipeline, which should look as follows:

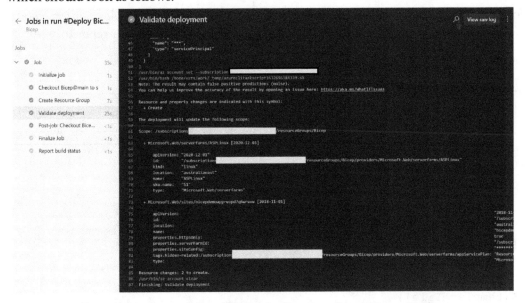

Figure 10.6 – Successfully validating the Bicep templates in Azure Pipeline

Now that we know that our validation was successful, we can go ahead and add the deployment step to our template.

Deploying the template

You are now ready to add the final step to deploy your template.

Adding the deployment step

You will need the following step for the deployment. It is your choice to either add this as a separate step or simply put it at the end of the validation step as an additional command:

```
- task: AzureCLI@2
  displayName: Validate deployment
  inputs:
    azureSubscription: $(azureServiceConnection)
    scriptType: bash
    scriptLocation: inlineScript
    inlineScript: |
      az deployment group create --name BicepDeployment
--resource-group $(resourceGroupName) --template-file
$(templateFile)
```

Note that we just had to replace what-if with create to be able to deploy our template in our step. You need to commit your new changes and push them to your repository.

You can also merge the steps to make your template a bit cleaner:

```
- task: AzureCLI@2
  displayName: Create Resource Group
  inputs:
    azureSubscription: $(azureServiceConnection)
    scriptType: bash
    scriptLocation: inlineScript
    inlineScript: |
      az group create --name $(resourceGroupName) --location
$(location)
      az deployment group create --name BicepDeployment
--resource-group $(resourceGroupName) --template-file
$(templateFile)
```

I have removed the validation step, but feel free to leave it there if you wish to validate your template before deployment. Now, we need to push our changes to our remote repository.

Pushing the changes to your repository

You need to run the same commands you used earlier with the proper commit message to commit and push your changes to your Azure repo:

```
git add .
git commit -m "Added the CLI task to deploy the template"
git push
```

Once you've done this, you should see a new deployment kick in and be completed. You can also verify your deployment in Azure by visiting your **Resource group** blade and checking the **Deployments** menu:

Figure 10.7 – Successful deployment verification in the Azure portal

We are almost there. The only other detail left is how to access the output of the deployment in our pipeline if we need it later in another step.

Accessing the deployment output in the pipeline

At times, you need to access one of the deployment outputs in the other steps in your pipeline. Perhaps you want to access the web app's URL to perform some automated tests, or a function app URL to be called later to seed some data. Regardless of the reason, you need to know how to access these outputs.

Receiving outputs from a deployment

You can use the Azure CLI or PowerShell to get the outputs from a deployment.
If you're using the Azure CLI, the following command would get the `appURL` output from our deployment:

```
az deployment group show \
  -g Bicep \
  -n BicepDeployment \
  --query properties.outputs.appURL.value
```

If you are running the preceding command in a PowerShell-based window, replace \ with '.

Using Azure PowerShell, the command would be as follows:

```
(Get-AzResourceGroupDeployment '
  -ResourceGroupName Bicep '
  -Name BicepDeployment).Outputs.appURL.value
```

Note that you need to replace the values for the resource group name and deployment name if you have changed them in the deployment step in your pipeline.

Now, you can assign this value to a variable in your pipeline and access it in other steps in the same job, or other jobs within the same run. If you are using PowerShell, you can use the following script to add `appURL` to the environment variables:

```
- task: AzurePowerShell@5
  displayName: Add outputs to environment variables
  inputs:
    azureSubscription: $(azureServiceConnection)
    scriptType: 'inlineScript'
    inline: |
```

```
    $appURL=(Get-AzResourceGroupDeployment -ResourceGroupName
Bicep -Name BicepDeployment).Outputs.appURL.value
    Write-Host "##vso[task.setvariable variable=APP_
URL;]$appURL"
    azurePowerShellVersion: latestVersion
```

This will install the Azure PowerShell module in the agent, get the value of the `appURL` output from the deployment, and set it as an environment variable called `APP_URL`.

Now, you can use this in your subsequent tasks by accessing the environment variables with the regular syntax of `$ENV:APP_URL`:

```
- task: PowerShell@2
  displayName: Use the environment variable
  inputs:
    targetType: 'inline'
    script: |
      Write-Host "The APP_URL environment variable value is
 '$Env:APP_URL'."
```

This should print the value of the output for you in your pipeline, as shown in the following screenshot:

```
Starting: Use the environment variable
==============================================================
Task         : PowerShell
Description  : Run a PowerShell script on Linux, macOS, or Windows
Version      : 2.190.0
Author       : Microsoft Corporation
Help         : https://docs.microsoft.com/azure/devops/pipelines/tasks/utility/powershell
==============================================================
Generating script.
======================== Starting Command Output ========================
/usr/bin/pwsh -NoLogo -NoProfile -NonInteractive -Command . '/home/vsts/work/_temp/b42deb7b-87b8-4c49-9189-4e1efc37d6ff.ps1'
The APP_URL environment variable value is 'appreopd7q6wravw.azurewebsites.net'. 
Finishing: Use the environment variable
```

Figure 10.8 – Accessing the environment variable set by outputs

You can find the complete pipeline code in the `Chapter10/completepipeline.yml` file in this book's GitHub repository. You can access the deployment output in other ways too, one of which will be explained in the next section at a high level.

An alternative approach to accessing deployment outputs

There is another way you can achieve the same outcome and that is to use the following procedure instead:

1. First, compile the Bicep file in your pipeline into an ARM template.

2. Then, deploy the ARM template using the `AzureResourceManagerTemplateDeployment@3` task and set the output using the `deploymentOutputs` property. You can find an example of using this task at `https://docs.microsoft.com/en-us/azure/azure-resource-manager/templates/add-template-to-azure-pipelines`.

3. Finally, access the output property in a PowerShell task and write it into an environment variable.

I will leave this as an exercise for you to do if you wish to try this approach instead. And that is all you need to deploy your Bicep templates using Azure DevOps. It is time to recap what you learned in this chapter.

Summary

In this chapter, you learned how to create an Azure DevOps organization and project, as well as how to create a service connection between that project and your Azure environment. Next, you followed a series of steps to create an Azure Pipeline from an existing YAML file.

Afterward, you learned how to add the necessary steps to create a resource group, validate your templates, and deploy them to your new resource group in Azure.

Finally, I explained two different approaches to accessing your deployment outputs and using them within your pipeline within the same stage, separate stage, or even in other pipelines. I hope you have enjoyed this book so far, but we are not there yet. In the next chapter, we will review how to deploy templates right from your GitHub repository using GitHub Actions.

11
Deploying Bicep Templates Using GitHub Actions

I must admit, you have come a long way. You now not only know how to create great Bicep templates but also how to deploy them from an Azure DevOps pipeline. But we cannot just leave it there; we must make sure you also know how to deploy your template from GitHub since the book's code snippets are in GitHub after all.

In this chapter, you will learn how to create a GitHub action that deploys your Bicep template in your Azure subscription. We will cover the following main topics:

- Creating a GitHub action
- Adding validation steps to the workflow
- Adding deployment steps to the workflow
- Using the official Azure ARM action
- Accessing deployment outputs for later use

Technical requirements

To take full advantage of this chapter, you will need to have access to a personal computer or laptop that has Visual Studio Code, its YAML extension, and Git installed. The code used throughout this chapter is stored in the GitHub repository at https://github.com/PacktPublishing/Infrastructure-as-Code-with-Azure-Bicep/tree/main/Chapter11.

Creating a GitHub action

GitHub Actions can help you automate, customize, and run workflows right from your repository. This will include a CI/CD pipeline since you already have access to your code and can leverage agents to run your workflow as you did in Azure DevOps in the last chapter. GitHub Actions also use YAML for implementing workflows; however, before we continue further, you need to take care of a few prerequisites first.

Prerequisites

You need a GitHub account to continue, which you can create for free at https://github.com/signup if you do not have one already. You also need to have access to an Azure account with an active subscription, which you can create for free at https://azure.microsoft.com/free.

You also need to create a service principal in your **Azure Active Directory**, which you can do easily using the following command:

```
az ad sp create-for-rbac --name GitHubActionApp --role
contributor --scopes /subscriptions/{subscription-id}/
resourceGroups/{MyResourceGroup} --sdk-auth
```

Replace {subscription-id} and {MyResourceGroup} with your subscription ID and resource group name before executing the command. The command should run successfully and give you a JSON object, which you need to capture for later use as follows:

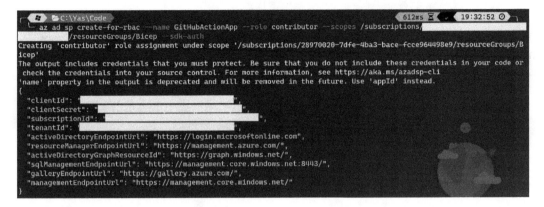

Figure 11.1 – Creating a service principal in Azure Active Directory for deployment

Now you need to push the code for this chapter into a GitHub repository. Follow these steps to do so:

1. Open a browser and navigate to github.com.

2. Log in to your account.

3. Click the ➕ button at the top right-hand corner and select a new repository.

4. Give it a name, select whether it is public or private, and click create.

You should see your repository's page with instructions on how to push your code to it, as follows:

Figure 11.2 – An empty GitHub repository

Now open a terminal and navigate to the Chapter11 folder of the book, then run the following commands (if you have cloned the repository, create an empty folder, and copy the files into it):

```
git init
git add .
git commit -m "Adding files to github"
git branch -m main
git remote add origin https://github.com/yashints/Bicep.git
git push -u origin main
```

Do not forget to replace the URL in the fifth command with your GitHub repository URL. And finally, you need to create a secret in your repository. Follow these steps to create one:

1. Click on the **Settings** menu.
2. Click **Secrets** in the left-hand side menu.
3. Click **New repository secret**.
4. Enter a name (AZURE_CREDENTIALS).
5. Paste the JSON object you got from creating a service principal into the value box as is.
6. Click **Add secret**.

You are now ready to create your workflow.

Creating the workflow from code

In the Chapter11 folder, there is a file called infra.yml, which you need to put inside a folder called .github/workflows. When you push your code up after creating this folder and putting the YAML file inside, it will automatically create a GitHub Action in your new repository. The file content should be as follows:

```
on: [push]
name: Deploy Bicep template
jobs:
  build-and-deploy:
    runs-on: ubuntu-latest
    steps:
      - uses: actions/checkout@main
      - name: Getting started
```

```
run:
    echo Hello from GitHub Actions
```

Once the run is finished, you should see a success message with **Hello from GitHub Actions** printed as follows:

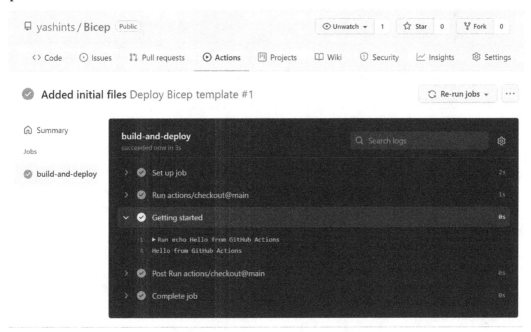

Figure 11.3 – GitHub Action run successfully

Now that you have the action ready, you can proceed to add the validation and deployment steps.

Adding validation steps to the workflow

Each action in your workflow can be a GitHub Action, which is created by someone else and published in the public marketplace, and so there is already an action that allows you to run Azure CLI commands. This will allow you to run the necessary commands to validate and deploy your template.

Adding an Azure CLI action to the workflow

The first thing you need to run the Azure CLI command is an action to log in to Azure. So go ahead and replace the `Getting started` command with the `azure/login` command:

```
- name: Azure Login
      uses: azure/login@v1
      with:
        creds: ${{ secrets.AZURE_CREDENTIALS }}
```

Now you can add an Azure CLI action to create your resource group and validate your template:

```
- name: Azure CLI script
      uses: azure/CLI@v1
      with:
        azcliversion: 2.0.72
        inlineScript: |
          az group create --name ${{ secrets.RG_NAME }}
--location ${{ secrets.LOCATION }}
          az deployment group what-if --name BicepDeployment
--resource-group ${{ secrets.RG_NAME }} --template-file main.
bicep
```

I have opted in to get the name of the resource group and its location from secrets also, but you can hardcode them or even go one level beyond that and use an environment. You can find more information at `https://docs.github.com/en/actions/security-guides/encrypted-secrets`.

It is now time to commit the code and push it up into your GitHub repository by running the following commands:

```
git add .
git commit -m "Added login and validation steps"
git push
```

The workflow should be automatically updated and triggered. Wait for the run to finish and you should see a success message like the following:

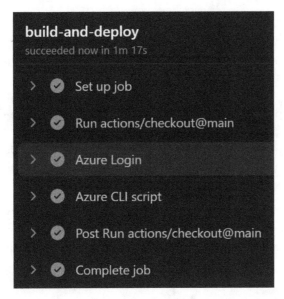

Figure 11.4 – Running Azure CLI commands in GitHub Actions

Now that the template is validated and is ready to be deployed, let's add the deployment command.

Adding deployment steps to the workflow

Adding the deployment command is as simple as replacing what-if with the create command. Your YAML file should look like this after all the changes:

```
on: [push]
name: Deploy Bicep template
jobs:
  build-and-deploy:
    runs-on: ubuntu-latest
    steps:
    - uses: actions/checkout@main
    - name: Azure Login
      uses: azure/login@v1
      with:
        creds: ${{ secrets.AZURE_CREDENTIALS }}
    - name: Validate and deploy the template
      uses: azure/CLI@v1
      with:
```

```
        azcliversion: 2.27.1
        inlineScript: |
          az group create --name ${{ secrets.RG_NAME }}
--location ${{ secrets.LOCATION }}
          az deployment group what-if --name BicepDeployment
--resource-group ${{ secrets.RG_NAME }} --template-file main.
bicep
          az deployment group create --name BicepDeployment
--resource-group ${{ secrets.RG_NAME }} --template-file main.
bicep
```

Add and commit your changes, then push them up into your repository. You should have a successful deployment, which can be verified by looking into your Azure resource group's **Deployment** blade. There is another way to deploy your template, which is easier, so let's review that too.

Using the official Azure ARM action

There is a GitHub action that is created for Bicep specifically and you can use it to deploy your templates. This action makes your workflow much cleaner too. You might be asking why I showed you the previous way, and the answer to that is that it is more in your control, and debugging might be easier for you if you are familiar with the Azure CLI.

Adding the Azure ARM action to the workflow

It is time to add the Azure ARM action to our workflow, so go ahead and delete the Azure CLI step and replace it with the following code snippet:

```
- name: deploy
    uses: azure/arm-deploy@v1
    with:
      subscriptionId: ${{ secrets.AZURE_SUBSCRIPTION }}
      resourceGroupName: ${{ secrets.RG_NAME }}
      template: ./main.bicep
      failOnStdErr: false
```

Now add, commit, and push the code up to your repository. The run will be successful; however, it will not make any changes in your Azure resource group since the deployments are incremental by default, meaning any existing resource will not change unless one of its changeable properties has been updated.

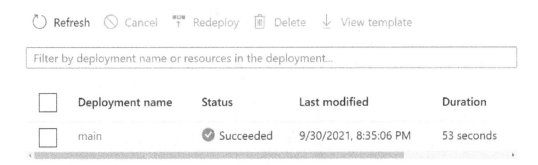

Figure 11.5 – Successful deployment using the Azure ARM action

Note that this step does validate the template and can receive parameters too. For more information about this action, please refer to its documentation at `https://github.com/Azure/arm-deploy`. It is now time to see how to access the template outputs in GitHub Actions.

Your complete YAML file should look like the following:

```yaml
on: [push]
name: Deploy Bicep template
jobs:
  build-and-deploy:
    runs-on: ubuntu-latest
    steps:
    - uses: actions/checkout@main
    - name: Azure Login
      uses: azure/login@v1
      with:
        creds: ${{ secrets.AZURE_CREDENTIALS }}

    - uses: azure/arm-deploy@v1
      id: deploy
      name: Deploy the template
      with:
        subscriptionId: ${{ secrets.AZURE_SUBSCRIPTION }}
        resourceGroupName: ${{ secrets.RG_NAME }}
        template: ./main.bicep
        failOnStdErr: false
```

Accessing deployment outputs for later use

It is worth mentioning again that you will face scenarios where you need to access your deployment output for many reasons, such as using it in the same pipeline in a later step, accessing it from another pipeline, or simply using it to find out about a property of a resource after it has been deployed for monitoring.

Accessing outputs from the Azure CLI action

If you are using the Azure CLI action, you can use the same approach we used in *Chapter 10, Deploying Bicep Using Azure DevOps*:

```
echo "BLOB_URL=$(az deployment group show -g ${{ secrets.RG_
NAME }} -n BicepDeployment --query properties.outputs.blobURL.
value -o tsv)" >> $GITHUB_ENV
```

This will create an environment variable called BLOB_URL, which you can access later using the regular GitHub syntax:

```
echo "${{ env.BLOB_URL }}"
```

Your complete step should look like this:

```
on: [push]
name: Deploy Bicep template
jobs:
  build-and-deploy:
    runs-on: ubuntu-latest
    steps:
    - uses: actions/checkout@main
    - name: Azure Login
      uses: azure/login@v1
      with:
        creds: ${{ secrets.AZURE_CREDENTIALS }}
    - name: Deploy
      run: |
        az group create --name ${{ secrets.RG_NAME }}
--location ${{ secrets.LOCATION }}
        az deployment group create --name BicepDeployment
--resource-group ${{ secrets.RG_NAME }} --template-file main.
bicep
```

```
        echo "BLOB_URL=$(az deployment group show -g ${{
secrets.RG_NAME }} -n BicepDeployment --query properties.
outputs.blobURL.value -o tsv)" >> $GITHUB_ENV
```

```
    - name: print env variable
      run: echo "${{ env.BLOB_URL }}"
```

The preceding code will print the blob URL of the storage account. Continue reading to find out how to access outputs from the Azure ARM action.

Accessing outputs from the Azure ARM action

If you have not used that approach and used the Azure ARM action instead, it will be a bit easier to get the outputs. Simply access the outputs of the previous step:

```
${{ steps.deploy.outputs.blobURL }}
```

In the preceding snippet, the deploy comes from an ID you have assigned to your step in our action. Your entire YAML file should look like the following:

```
on: [push]
name: Deploy Bicep template
jobs:
  build-and-deploy:
    runs-on: ubuntu-latest
    steps:
    - uses: actions/checkout@main
    - name: Azure Login
      uses: azure/login@v1
      with:
        creds: ${{ secrets.AZURE_CREDENTIALS }}

    - uses: azure/arm-deploy@v1
      id: deploy
      name: Deploy the template
      with:
        subscriptionId: ${{ secrets.AZURE_SUBSCRIPTION }}
        resourceGroupName: ${{ secrets.RG_NAME }}
        template: ./main.bicep
```

```
        failOnStdErr: false
 - name: Echo blob URL
    run: |
      echo ${{ steps.deploy.outputs.blobURL }}
```

If you commit and push the code, you should see the success message and the blob URL shown in the output like the following:

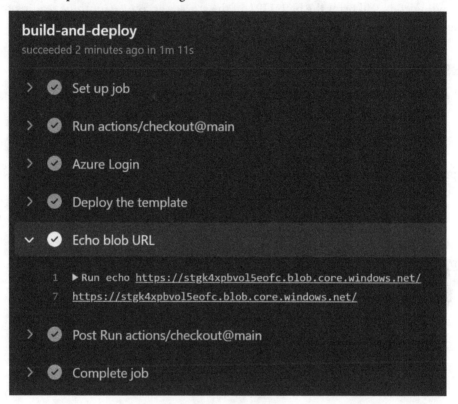

Figure 11.6 – Accessing deployment output from the Azure ARM action

With that, you should now be confident to use both Azure DevOps and GitHub Actions to deploy your Bicep templates.

Finally, the complete workflow files are in the Chapter11 folder in our GitHub repository for your reference, AzureCLI.yml for our first approach and AzureARM. yml for our second approach. But try to follow along instead of copying those files and using them from the beginning. Let's now recap what you have learned in this chapter.

Summary

In this chapter, you learned how to create a GitHub Action workflow from a YAML file in your source code repository. You learned how to create a service principal and create secrets in your repository to be accessed within your GitHub Action.

Then you saw how to add the necessary steps to validate and deploy your templates using two different actions, the Azure CLI and Azure ARM. We finished the chapter with two different ways to access the output of our deployment templates, both via environment variables and outputs of the previous step.

You now should be very proud to have come so far, but we have just a few more points to review before jumping into our editors and starting to write our templates. In our last chapter, we will review some best practices that will help you to really stand out from the crowd when it comes to infrastructure as code. So continue to find out more – you are nearly there.

12
Exploring Best Practices for Future Maintenance

This is the last chapter of this book, and I am very happy you are reading it. This means you now know how to create great templates and help your team deploy your infrastructure via code with great confidence.

However, there are a few more topics we need to go through to make sure you always keep yourself and your team ahead of the curve since, in the cloud world, everything moves faster than any other industry. We will cover topics including best practices in IaC, idempotency in deployments, modularity, and some best practices when it comes to Bicep. We will finish this chapter by pointing out the current limitations in Bicep that you need to take into consideration.

In this chapter, we are going to cover the following main topics:

- Applying version control and code flows for your IaC
- Idempotency and its importance
- Modularity and microservices

- Bicep best practices
- Managing service version updates
- Azure Bicep limitations

Technical requirements

This chapter does not have any technical requirements. You can find the samples code for this chapter at `https://github.com/PacktPublishing/Infrastructure-as-Code-with-Azure-Bicep/tree/main/Chapter12`.

Applying version control and code flows for your IaC

When it comes to IaC, there are many patterns you can leverage. We will review the two most important ones and review the pros and cons of each.

Single pipeline approach

The first approach is to put all the steps to deploy the infrastructure and code in the same pipeline. This has some benefits, such as making sure the environments and code are compatible by testing the IaC before deployment, which gives you great confidence in the result.

However, this has some drawbacks, including the fact that every time there is a code change or a change in the environment, all the steps will run, which makes every run longer than it should be. This also means that pull request validations will take longer, so you might feel a little slowness in your developers getting tasks done.

Separate pipelines for code and infrastructure

A much better approach is to have separate pipelines for code and infrastructure. This means that code changes will only trigger a pipeline and changes to cloud resources will only trigger its pipeline.

Another great aspect of this approach is the speed of testing and deployment since everything is separate. You will need to make some extra effort to implement this approach by using some extra configuration for your pipelines, such as a path filter and trigger exclusions, but I can assure you that the result is worth it.

There are some drawbacks to this approach too, which include more work upfront and deployment complexity. If you need to access the infrastructure deployment outputs in your code pipeline, you need to add some extra tasks and use one of the approaches we talked about in the last two chapters.

It also makes it difficult to make sure cloud resource changes do not break the application or vice versa, which requires integration testing to be written. But again, the result will make your team agile, confident, and in full control of the environment.

Source control everything

Last, we would not be talking about pipelines if we did not have source control in place. Having your templates in source control makes it easier to keep track of the changes that have been applied and roll back to a previous good state in case of failure. Apart from that, the reusability that is created will let other teams within your organization benefit from collaboration with your team and vice versa. Now that we have talked about IaC, it is time to review idempotency in your deployments.

Idempotency and its importance

Idempotency means no matter how many times you run your pipeline or what the current state of your cloud resources is, you always get the same result at the end of your deployments.

Idempotency

For example, if your template is deploying a storage account in the first run, and then an additional storage account if you run it again, it is not idempotent. It is very important to keep your deployment idempotent to prevent any change in behavior, which makes troubleshooting a nightmare.

Immutability

Immutability is also something that you need to consider. Not only it is important to make sure your templates provide the same result at each run, but the configuration of your resources must be maintained if no change has been recorded.

These issues usually happen when you are not as confident about your cloud deployment as you are about your code and as such, your applications might suffer from slow memory, run out of disk space, and more. To prevent this, you need to make sure your resources are immutable, which means instead of modifying your existing resources, you must deploy a set of new resources.

Of course, this is not applicable in every scenario, especially since it usually requires provisioning additional resources to route the traffic accordingly if a resource is replaced with a new one.

Modularity and microservices

Modularizing your templates is essential, especially if your cloud environment is complex. This will help your code be more maintainable, your templates more readable, and resource ownership easier.

Imagine an organization with different teams for networking and applications. If each team takes ownership of their corresponding resources, the risk of any misconfiguration or incorrect resource structure will be minimized. Keep in mind that this will not undermine the concept of cross-functional teams, since the point here is keeping resources in modules that are related and can be deployed together. Furthermore, it may only be the templates that are generated by the corresponding team and shared for other teams for reuse for their deployments.

This will also make your templates easier to read since you now have references to modules instead of repeating your code over and over again. Not only that, but it also makes your templates a long and hard-to-maintain document, which scares every developer in your team when it comes to making any changes to it.

Apart from that, this approach makes it easier for you to implement a microservice architecture since you can break down your apps into smaller services and reuse the module to deploy them.

Now, it's time to review some best practices in Bicep that will help you create better templates and modules.

Bicep best practices

Like any other IaC tool, Bicep requires some discipline to make sure that if you look at your templates in a few years, when the original developers might have left the team, the new members can still read and modify them without any issues.

Parameters

Starting with parameters, the very first recommendation is to choose a good naming convention, document it, and stick to it. Make sure your resource names are clear, it's easy to pinpoint their role, and they are easy to find. Keep all the parameter definitions at the top of the template to make it easier to review, add, or remove them in the future. You can also refer to `https://docs.microsoft.com/en-us/azure/cloud-adoption-framework/ready/azure-best-practices/resource-naming` to find some of the most used conventions and best practices published by Microsoft.

Limit the values for your parameters using the `@allowed` decorator to reduce the risk of a user passing an invalid or impractical value to your template. Provide a minimum and a maximum for those parameters where there are limitations enforced by Azure to prevent any errors at runtime and catch them upfront.

Variables

Similarly, use a good naming convention for variables, define them where applicable and where they are easy to find, and use functions for more complex formulas rather than inline expressions. Also, use camel case for their naming to make reading them easy and coming up with one easier.

Use the `uniqueString()` function to generate unique values for your variables instead of trying to come up with a random value yourself, which increases the risk of facing an issue later.

Resource definitions

When you're defining your resources, choose a good naming convention for symbolic names too. Try avoiding complex expressions and use variables or functions for those situations. If you are using resource properties later, try not to populate them yourself. Instead, use their output properties, which give you the exact values.

When possible, avoid the `reference` and `referenceId` functions and use symbolic names instead. Use the `existing` keyword if your resource has not been created in this template, and then use the symbolic name to access its properties in the child or dependent resources.

Avoid nesting too many resources, bring them to the top level, and set their parents using symbolic names. This makes your template much easier to read and maintain.

Outputs

Avoid outputting sensitive information such as keys and secrets. Only output what might be used later in your pipeline or other dependent ones. Choose a naming convention for your outputs too and stick to it. If you need to access the properties of previously created resources, use the existing keyword, and define them in your template. They will not be created in your ARM template but they will make your job and reading your template much easier.

Configuration set

Rather than defining lots of individual parameters, create predefined sets of variables and select the one you need during your deployments. For example, imagine that we need different **SKUs** for production versus non-production resources. You can create a variable such as the following:

```
var environmentConfigurationMap = {
  Production: {
    appServicePlan: {
      sku: {
        name: 'P2V3'
        capacity: 3
      }
    }
    appServiceApp: {
      alwaysOn: false
    }
  }
  NonProduction: {
    appServicePlan: {
      sku: {
        name: 'S2'
        capacity: 1
      }
    }
    appServiceApp: {
      alwaysOn: false
    }
```

```
    }
}
```

Then, pass a single parameter that defines which environment is being deployed. Based on the value of this parameter, choose the corresponding part of the variable:

```
@allowed([
   'Production'
   'NonProduction'
])
param environmentType string = 'NonProduction'
resource appServicePlan 'Microsoft.Web/serverfarms@2020-06-01'
= {
  name: appServicePlanName
  location: location
  sku: environmentConfigurationMap[environmentType].
appServicePlan.sku
}
```

With this approach, you will not need to depend on the user to know which SKU to use for which environment, and everything is kept simple and effective in your source control. Just try to group the properties by resource to simplify the definitions. This enables you to define both individual property values and object values.

You can mix this approach with resource conditions to create even more powerful templates.

Shared variable file

Instead of repeating variables in each template when they need to be shared, try loading them from a shared JSON file within your template. This approach simplifies your template even more and allows you to keep a single source of truth for your variables.

To use this approach, simply create a JSON file like the following:

```
{
    "storageAccountPrefix": "stg",
    "appServicePrefix": "myapp"
}
```

Then, in your template, use the json function in combination with the loadTextContent function to load the file. Then, simply access the variables defined in the file:

```
var sharedNamePrefixes = json(loadTextContent('./shared-
prefixes.json'))
```

```
var appServiceAppName = '${sharedNamePrefixes.
appServicePrefix}-${uniqueString(resourceGroup().id)}'
```

```
var storageAccountName = '${sharedNamePrefixes.
storageAccountPrefix}myapp${uniqueString(resourceGroup().id)}'
```

Keep in mind that when you use this approach, the JSON file will be included within the ARM template, and with the maximum file size being 4 MB, it is important to use it wisely and when necessary.

Managing service version updates

Microsoft Azure is always changing for the better. Services get updated and new versions get released, sometimes daily. To keep yourself ahead of these changes, you can use the Azure Updates tool to subscribe to and receive any update that is made to Azure services as soon as possible. You can find the tool at https://azure.microsoft.com/en-us/updates/.

This will allow you to have control and make informed decisions on which version of the service to use in your Bicep templates.

Microsoft publishes best practices that get updated as the product evolves. You can read more on this at https://docs.microsoft.com/en-us/azure/azure-resource-manager/bicep/best-practices.

Azure Bicep's known limitations

Like any other tool, Bicep has some limitations, and considering how new it is, it does make sense for some of these issues to have not been addressed yet. So, let's see what these limitations are and where to find more information about them.

Single-line objects and arrays

The first known limitation is that there is no support for single-line objects and arrays. You might have used an array to create multiple resources using `copy` in your ARM templates, in which case you would have passed an array parameter (that is, `['a', 'b', 'c']`). You cannot have the same in Bicep, but this can be done using a new line:

```
allowed: [
   'Basic'
   'Standard'
   'Premium'
]
```

Work is in progress to add support for this, and you can find updates in their GitHub repository at `https://github.com/Azure/bicep/issues/498`.

Newline sensitivity

Bicep lang is newline-sensitive, which means that if you accidentally insert a new line in your file, the interpretation will be different. Let's see what this means by looking at an example. Say you want to write an `if` condition to create a variable value. You might write it like so:

```
var value = myParam == 'value1' ? settingsTable.value1 :
              myParam == 'value2' ? settingsTable.value2 :
                {}
```

If you use this code snippet in your Bicep file, you will get a compilation error since this means something completely different in Bicep. In Bicep, you need to write this in a single line:

```
var value = myParam == 'value1' ? settingsTable.value1 :
myParam == 'value2' ? settingsTable.value2 : {}
```

> **Note**
> Do not pay attention to how the correct form is wrapped – this is just because of a lack of horizontal space on this page.

This was supposed to be on the v0.2 milestone but it got moved up to v0.5 later. You can find more information on their GitHub issue at `https://github.com/Azure/bicep/issues/146`.

No support for API profiles

API profiles specify the Azure resource provider and its API version, which should be used on the ARM REST endpoints. Using this feature, you can create different clients in different languages, which will use different versions of APIs. This might be for backward compatibility reasons or simply being behind the latest version. Did this sound complex? Let me clarify by providing an example. Normally, you would need the resource type and its API version to tell ARM what to create:

```
'microsoft.compute/virtualMachines@2020-06-01'
```

This is important for Azure Resource Manager, but why confuse users when you can simplify it if they do not care what version is used to create their resource?

```
'microsoft.compute/virtualMachines' => virtualMachines or vm
```

Azure Bicep does not support this yet and the team is working on it. However, they have mentioned that it might be implemented differently in Bicep since it is more complex than it looks. You can find more information on their GitHub issue at `https://github.com/Azure/bicep/issues/622`.

CLI limitations

For now, there are two temporary limitations with the CLI and they only occur during compilation. The first is that templates that use `copy` cannot be decompiled. The other is the templates that use nested templates can *only* be decompiled if they are using the `inner` expression evaluation scope. If you are not familiar with this concept, do not worry about it – I will give you an example to make it clear what this limitation is about.

When using nested templates, you can explicitly specify whether the expressions are evaluated at the parent or child level using the `expressionEvaluationOptions` flag:

```
{
  "type": "Microsoft.Resources/deployments",
  "apiVersion": "2020-10-01",
  "name": "nestedTemplate1",
  "properties": {
    "expressionEvaluationOptions": {
      "scope": "inner"
    },
    ...
```

And that is all you need to add to your templates to transpile them successfully. However, keep in mind that the scope has changed for your variables, so you might need to make the necessary adjustments. Now, it's time to recap what we reviewed in this chapter and wrap up this book.

To find out more about these limitations and keep up to date, go to `https://docs.microsoft.com/en-us/azure/azure-resource-manager/bicep/overview#known-limitations`.

Summary

In this chapter, we discussed many topics, from IaC best practices to what idempotency and immutability are when it comes to IaC. This was followed by an overview of modularity and how it helps you implement microservices patterns, and then some of the best practices when it comes to Bicep that cover ideas and industry standards as regards the use of parameters, variables, resources, outputs, and some useful patterns such as configuration settings and variables files.

Finally, we reviewed some of the known limitations of Azure Bicep since the tool is new and it is natural for some of these to have not been addressed yet.

I am so glad that you have come so far reading this book. Hopefully, it has helped you not only get started with Bicep but become an expert in creating reusable, modular templates, which will help your team and others in your organization. If anything changes in this space, I will make sure to update this book, so keep an eye out for some upcoming announcements.

Index

workflow
    Azure ARM action, adding to 178
    Azure CLI action, adding to 176, 177
    creating, from code 174, 175
    deployment step, adding to 177, 178
    validation step, adding to 175

Packt.com

Subscribe to our online digital library for full access to over 7,000 books and videos, as well as industry leading tools to help you plan your personal development and advance your career. For more information, please visit our website.

Why subscribe?

- Spend less time learning and more time coding with practical eBooks and Videos from over 4,000 industry professionals

- Improve your learning with Skill Plans built especially for you

- Get a free eBook or video every month

- Fully searchable for easy access to vital information

- Copy and paste, print, and bookmark content

Did you know that Packt offers eBook versions of every book published, with PDF and ePub files available? You can upgrade to the eBook version at packt.com and as a print book customer, you are entitled to a discount on the eBook copy. Get in touch with us at customercare@packtpub.com for more details.

At www.packt.com, you can also read a collection of free technical articles, sign up for a range of free newsletters, and receive exclusive discounts and offers on Packt books and eBooks.

Other Books You May Enjoy

If you enjoyed this book, you may be interested in these other books by Packt:

Azure for Architects

Ritesh Modi, Jack Lee, and Rithin Skaria

ISBN: 978-1-83921-586-5

- Understand the components of the Azure cloud platform
- Use cloud design patterns
- Use enterprise security guidelines for your Azure deployment
- Design and implement serverless and integration solutions
- Build efficient data solutions on Azure
- Understand container services on Azure

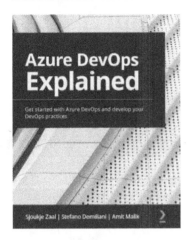

Azure DevOps Explained

Sjoukje Zaal | Stefano Demiliani | Amit Malik

ISBN: 978-1-80056-351-3

- Get to grips with Azure DevOps
- Find out about project management with Azure Boards
- Understand source code management with Azure Repos
- Build and release pipelines
- Run quality tests in build pipelines
- Use artifacts and integrate Azure DevOps in the GitHub flow
- Discover real-world CI/CD scenarios with Azure DevOps

Packt is searching for authors like you

If you're interested in becoming an author for Packt, please visit `authors.packtpub.com` and apply today. We have worked with thousands of developers and tech professionals, just like you, to help them share their insight with the global tech community. You can make a general application, apply for a specific hot topic that we are recruiting an author for, or submit your own idea.

Share Your Thoughts

Once you've read *Infrastructure as Code with Azure Bicep*, we'd love to hear your thoughts! Please `click here to go straight to the Amazon review page` for this book and share your feedback.

Your review is important to us and the tech community and will help us make sure we're delivering excellent quality content.

Printed in the USA
CPSIA information can be obtained
at www.ICGtesting.com
LVHW080809221023
761509LV00026B/40